THE FAITH
OF THE APOSTLES' CREED

THE FAITH OF
THE APOSTLES' CREED

AN ESSAY IN ADJUSTMENT OF BELIEF AND FAITH

BY

J. F. BETHUNE-BAKER, D.D.

LADY MARGARET'S READER IN DIVINITY IN THE
UNIVERSITY OF CAMBRIDGE

WIPF & STOCK · Eugene, Oregon

Wipf and Stock Publishers
199 W 8th Ave, Suite 3
Eugene, OR 97401

The Faith of the Apostles' Creed
An Essay in Adjustment of Belief and Faith
By Bethune-Baker, J.F.
Softcover ISBN-13: 978-1-6667-6450-5
Hardcover ISBN-13: 978-1-6667-6451-2
eBook ISBN-13: 978-1-6667-6452-9
Publication date 11/10/2022
Previously published by
Macmillan and Co., Limited, 1918

This edition is a scanned facsimile of the original edition
published in 1918.

DEDICATED

IN LOYAL HOMAGE

TO

THE LADY MARGARETE

(✝ 29 JUNE MDIX)

A DEVOUT CHRISTIAN OF THE OLD SCHOOL
WHO FOUNDED PROFESSORSHIPS AND COLLEGES
TO FOSTER THE NEW LEARNING OF HER TIME

AND TO

AN OTHER LADY

NO LESS DEVOTED TO CHRISTIAN IDEALS

WHO DESIRES TO HAVE SET FORTH

IN THE VULGAR TONGUE OF TO-DAY

THE FAITH OF A CHRISTIAN

ACCORDING TO THE APOSTLES' CREED

. . . she that ordeyned two contynuall Reders in both the Unyversytyes to teche the holy Dyvynyte of Jhesu.—*A Mornynge Remembraunce*, compyled by the Reverent Fader in God, Johann Fysher, Bishop of Rochester.

ἵνα μὴ λέγω σοι ὅτι καὶ ἐμαυτόν σοι προσοφείλω.

O Timothy, guard that which is committed unto thee.—1 TIM. vi. 20.

And he gave them ten pounds, and said unto them, Trade ye herewith till I come.—LUKE xix. 13.

I came that they might have life and have it in abundance.—JOHN x. 10.

PREFACE

It is not easy to define the Faith of a Christian.[1] If a 'Christian' is a disciple of Jesus, a member of His school, he clearly ought to share His faith. He ought to have the same attitude to life and the same beliefs about the true relations of GOD to the world and to men, and of men to one another, as Jesus had. This faith of Jesus about GOD and the potentialities and destiny of Man, and the meaning of the Universe

[1] The title of this book, to which it was actually written, was *The Faith of a Christian according to the Apostles' Creed*. Messrs. Macmillan & Co., however, have already published a book entitled *The Faith of a Christian, by a Disciple*, which has had a large circulation (First Edition 1904, Sixpenny Edition 1905, Shilling Edition 1913), though I was not myself acquainted with it. The title of my own book has therefore been changed, but I have not thought it necessary to alter the text. The author of *The Faith of a Christian*, the Rev. Bernard Lucas, speaks in his Preface of the different idioms in which men must express their faith. My idiom is not quite the same as his, but he gives voice to my own profound conviction when he suggests that the more idioms the language of Religion possesses the better for Religion; and my own 'idiomatic' commentary on the Apostles' Creed would never have been written unless its author could say of it, as Mr. Lucas said of his book—"In the belief that his idiom may be helpful to others of like mind, he sends it upon its mission, with grateful acknowledgements for the help he has received from the masters who have taught him, and with the hope that to some at least it may speak in their own tongue of those divine mysteries which must for ever transcend all utterance."

and Life, ought to be at least part of the Faith of a Christian :—even if he does not share it in every particular, he ought to be able to justify any departure from it, and to shew that his central religious convictions are the same as those of Jesus, and that apparent variations are not real divergences. Jesus is his 'master', and the disciple must be loyal to his master's dominant ideas.

It is true that the very name 'Christian' implies something more than this. It implies the belief that Jesus was the Messiah ; and the Faith of a Christian is thus linked on to some of the chief conceptions of the Religion of Israel and the hopes of its poets and prophets.

The name 'Christian' denotes one who not only shares the beliefs of Jesus but has a particular kind of belief about Him and in Him, as being the Person appointed to fulfil those hopes of Israel, though on a grander scale and in other ways than Israel itself had expected. A Christian is one who trusts in Jesus as the Deliverer of the world, the Saviour of mankind, according to the will and purpose of GOD, appointed by Him to reveal that purpose and to shew the way in which it must be fulfilled : to be Himself in His own Person the potential fulfilment of it for all men. That is a high doctrine about Him. But some who held it of old felt that it did not exhaust the significance of His Person or supply a full explanation of the religious experience which they had through Him. They were assured that through their association with Him they were brought into a new and intimate association with GOD, and by steps which cannot be traced exactly they came to regard Him who was the medium of this new consciousness as Himself Divine, the pre-existent Son of GOD who had divested Himself of the riches of His Divine estate and humbled Himself to be born of a woman and enter on human life and become the servant of men. Or, if they thought in the terms of the noblest religious philosophy of their time, they conceived Him as the manifestation in space and time, under the conditions of human life, of the eternal Reason or the infinite Wisdom or the secret Purpose of GOD, bringing the Divine activity, which had hitherto worked invisibly in the world and men, into visible and immediate operation —its very embodiment, making it for the first time fully effective in the world. It was long before the details of this doctrine of the Incarnation were worked out. It is conceivable, of course, that some other category might have served to express the early Christian conviction that the impact of Jesus on the world was the impact of GOD Himself, that in His personality and life there was given a revelation of the personality and life of GOD. It is conceivable that Christians of a future age may yet find some other category that will express more exactly for them, in closer correspondence with their knowledge of the universe and of life, what their early forefathers meant by the Incarnation. Categories of thought may change while continuity of faith is kept. But it would appear that no one who does not retain the conviction that found expression in the doctrine of the Incarnation can ever justly call himself a Christian.

Yet, as the new Religion of the new experience and consciousness grew and developed, and the new People of GOD spread themselves out in the world, they not only retained many of the old ideas they had had before they were 'Christian', but they also absorbed many new ones derived from various outside sources. And so 'Christianity'—the religion of the organized Christian Society—as a historical phenomenon has been, and is, an amalgamation of ideas and institutions many of which are in no sense specifically Christian, and have not been, even by adoption, more than superficially Christianized. Obviously they are not Christian simply because Christians have accepted them and the Church has wrought them into her system. On the contrary, some of them at least are symptoms rather of the failure of Christians to understand and realize the full scope of their Faith. The student of the history knows that they came in both from above and from

PREFACE

below[1]: some of them, as it were, imposed on the thought of the Church by the 'superior' authority of learned men habituated to the ideas of the pre-Christian schools of philosophy, and never more than dimly understood by the rank and file of the Church; and others of them having their origin in the untutored emotions of the masses and, because they seemed to support the supernatural basis of the Church, winning the sanction of the learned, with the result that " later theology is largely occupied with providing a basis in Scripture and philosophy for opinions which have no real connexion with either the one or the other ".[2] Yet all alike they have permeated the tradition which many Christians deem it a

---

[1] An example of the former class of ideas that worked downwards from above is seen in the theory of the impassibility of GOD, which not only makes havoc of the doctrine of the Incarnation, but is also responsible for the chaotic condition to which the doctrine of the Person of Christ was reduced by the theory that He suffered *qua* man but not *qua* GOD, and at one and the same time was ignorant of things *qua* man while knowing everything *qua* GOD. As regards the latter class of ideas that worked upwards from below, it may indeed be questioned whether 'Christianity' has ever been free from the kind of belief in the supernatural which allows for no science of Nature and none of that regularity of the operation of the forces at work in the Universe on the assumption of which all the Natural Sciences are based. It is possibly to this kind of belief working upwards from below that some of the narratives of the Gospels are due. But it was certainly the sensationalism of the least educated masses of the community (seen in much pre-Christian popular piety) that led to the naturalization in the Church and its institutions of the frame of mind that gave to Christianity of later times the character which made it inevitably a drag on the progress of knowledge of the Universe.

[2] C. Bigg, *Wayside Sketches*, pp. 50 ff.

pious duty to guard and hand on unaltered, because it was once 'delivered to the Saints'.

It has, however, always been the claim of the Church that in all its Creeds and other formularies it was only expressing and safeguarding the primitive convictions of Christians as they were reflected in the various books of the New Testament; new terms were used simply to sum up the sense of Scripture, in relation to new ideas which seemed to run counter to the tradition. It is equally true that for most Christians in the past these primitive convictions have been so closely associated with belief in the complete historical exactitude of the narratives of the Gospels that where this belief is shaken or in suspense the convictions themselves seem to be discredited. Yet it is not impossible to read some of those narratives, not as exact representations in word of the thing that actually happened, but rather as interpretations of experiences that beggared description. When read in this way, they can and do become to men and women of to-day the medium of the same convictions of faith as they have produced when treated as literally historical. This power is one, no doubt, which they have in common with all great literature of the imagination, but they have it to a unique degree; and the personality, the character and life, that gradually grows up before the reader, as the cumulative effect of the various narratives, is known to be no imaginative creation but that of one who actually lived as man the life of men. The Person thus depicted, the subject and the centre of unique experience, stands out as Himself unique. The reader is drawn into the circle of the same experience; he sees and knows for himself. This is the real, as it is the uniquely convincing, evidence of the Gospels. And to one who has reached these convictions, the question whether the narratives give an exact account of the way in which things happened or were done, or not, becomes a question of merely scientific or antiquarian interest. It has nothing to do with religion. Whether the Person who has won his allegiance was born of a Virgin Mother or not; whether He could walk on water, or feed a multitude with a few loaves and fishes, or blast a fig-tree with a word, or clothe Himself with a visible body after His death, or not; whether disease is the work of demons or of microbes:—these are not questions on the answer to which the religious convictions of a Christian depend. We have learnt not to search the Old Testament Scriptures for a revelation of the facts and principles of Natural Science: we shall learn in time to disentangle our Christian convictions of Faith from the scientific beliefs of any particular era of human knowledge or theory, whether it be the first century or the twentieth or the twenty-first.

It is just this process of disentanglement which has given its special character to the modern period in the history of Christian Theology—the period which does not begin till late in the seventeenth century, for 'modern' ideas had no part in the theology of the Reformation, and have only recently become at all naturalized within the Church.[1] The slowness which the Church has shewn in admitting them to any part in the restatement of its system of doctrines is one of the chief causes of the alienation from its fellowship of many who share its highest moral and spiritual convictions and ideals. But the leaven of the new knowledge which in

[1] It is worth while to recall the fact that the Articles of the Church of England, which are still subscribed by the Clergy, belong to the pre-Copernican period of knowledge of the world in which we live. They were drawn up for the most part only ten years after the first printed copy of the great work which was to revolutionize our conceptions of the universe was put into the hands of its author Copernicus on his death-bed (1543). Nearly a hundred years more had to pass before the line of investigation which he originated was made effective by the work of Kepler (1609) and Galileo (the book for which he was condemned was published in 1632), and some fifty years more before our own Newton's *Principia* was published (1687). And the new knowledge did not spread rapidly; while, for the complete disintegration of the old scholastic theology within the Church itself, the still newer knowledge of the nineteenth century was needed. That the system as such can ever be reintegrated I do not believe. It must be a new system that takes its place, and a system founded on 'presuppositions' other than those by the help of which the traditional Theology was built up. It will distinguish between Christian Faith and ecclesiastical tradition.

other departments has ousted the old knowledge, or the new method and the new theory which takes the place of the old, has been working none the less effectively because it has rarely been perceptible; and could the voice of the Church of England as a whole become articulate, could its instructed but usually silent mind find adequate expression, it would, I am sure, reveal a state of suspense of judgement as to such questions as I have mentioned and a refusal to treat them as questions of primary importance. It is not needed, perhaps, that the Church should formally, or explicitly, repudiate primitive beliefs or old points of view. But there is an ever-growing and insistent demand within the Church itself that individuals, whether of the clergy or of the laity, shall not be debarred from free investigation, from fresh angles of vision, of all such beliefs and opinions, and free expression of the conclusions which they reach, without charges of disloyalty or infringement of their rights of fellowship in the Church. And there is also, I am sure, an equally resolute determination—far more widespread than is publicly known—that such old beliefs as the birth of our Lord from a Virgin and His resurrection in the body which was laid in the tomb shall not be treated as of the essence of the Faith of a Christian. In this era of transition from an old order to a new, when there is a spirit abroad that questions all existing institutions and conventions, and at the same time a new outpouring of the spirit of Christian brotherhood and moral aspiration, it is surely no time to treat as aliens from the Christian Faith those who accept the Lordship of Christ, His ideals of GOD and life, as pourtrayed in the Gospels, and desire to live in the fellowship of the ordered Christian Society, to share in its worship and serve in its ministry, pledged to promote the conception of GOD and of Man of which the doctrine of the Incarnation is the expression, and the primitive Christian experience, and the continuous religious consciousness of Christians ever since, the guarantee. The tradition in the Church of England is that those who cannot live at peace in its fellowship go out or drop away. The loss to the Church, and to some of them, has been grievous. But no school can have a monopoly of the Church. Those who desire one must either moderate their greed, or go. The so-called 'modernists' within the Church to-day will not go out, for they want no monopoly. Nor will they be muzzled and let their case go against them by default. They have already given proof of that. They will not be so disloyal to the great religious tradition they have inherited as to allow the spacious Church of the English people—the only Catholic Church in the world—to be robbed

PREFACE

of its distinctive glory as the Church in which "Faith is not afraid to reason, nor Reason to adore":—the Church always, generation after generation, of 'the old faith' and 'the new learning'. If they make the task of the champions of the authority of the tradition harder, that is not their fault, nor ought it to be regarded as a misfortune by those champions. "He that is not against us is for us", and in the things of the spirit that really matter modernist and traditionalist are agreed. They are agreed as to the spiritual verities or realities which the Creed of the Church affirms.

My exposition of the Apostles' Creed only aims at indicating, in terms as general as possible, what the religious values of its various clauses are. But before entering on it I must refer to some recent discussions of the subject.

When the War broke on us in August 1914 we were already in the midst of a controversy in matters of life and death to the Church of England, and through it to the Religion of the Nation. An attempt had been made to destroy the peculiar genius of the Church of England, to arrest its freedom of movement and self-adaptation, to prevent it from coming to terms with much of the best religious thought and activity of the times, to narrow arbitrarily its natural process of expansion, to curtail the comprehensiveness which has always been its strength, and to capture its organization and its official machinery in the interests of one of the several groups, or schools of thought, of which the Church has always been composed. This group had proclaimed in arrogant tones that it could not live with the others : it could not tolerate their presence in the same communion with themselves. There was indeed a lull at the moment. It seemed as if a *modus vivendi*, a fair working arrangement, could be found. But the Church Congress, which was to have met in September, would have been the occasion of further discussion, as the result of which some of the issues would have been clearer to the people of England than they were.

The War broke on us, and by general consent a kind of *trève de Dieu* was established about all matters that did not directly concern the greater issues which were involved in the War. There could be no battle for justice and freedom and brotherhood between different temperaments and schools within the Church of England, the Church of the English people, while the cause of justice and freedom and brotherhood between the nations and peoples of the whole world was at stake and hung trembling in the balance.

The ideals of life which we knew were Christian in essence, about which we were all agreed, were threatened ; and as we realized this at once, or came to realize it in the first few months of the War, we knew that all our strength must be exerted in defence of the greater cause. Perhaps the war of defence would so bring us face to face with reality that we should discern the things of the spirit, the deep things of GOD, with clearer eyes, and form a truer estimate than before of the real content and values of life. We should ever after be able to put first things first.

That the experience of the last three years has had this effect in the case of hundreds of thousands of men and women of all classes within the community I cannot doubt. All kinds of barriers have disappeared, and even if party organizations remain, party shibboleths, social, economic, and political, have lost their meaning. Tyrannies and autocracies of every description are tumbling down. 'Freedom', indeed, as we have had it, has been curtailed, and a discipline unknown before established in the State. But the discipline which the people of England are bearing, severe and searching as it is, they bear as a discipline self-imposed, and they will not bear it a day longer than it has their free consent; nor will they tolerate in peace-time restrictions of freedom save such as are necessary to safeguard a free community from those who would shatter its unity of spirit.

Only in matters ecclesiastical has this unity of

the spirit been visibly and flagrantly broken, and those who would gladly live in the bond of peace with their fellow-Churchmen, and join with them and their other fellow-Christians in championing the great spiritual convictions of our common Faith, are assailed again as they were in 1914 and obliged to defend the cause of Freedom in the Church that is again endangered.[1]

We have all heard that in war a strong offensive is often the best form of defence, and the position of our assailants in the Church is in many respects peculiarly vulnerable. But they are our fellow-Churchmen and we have no desire to shew up inconsistencies, to dwell on what seem to us intellectual insincerities, or even to strip off the *camouflage* (often perhaps unintentional) with which some of their aims are disguised. Criticism of that kind is easy, yet at its best it is a very imperfect method of seeking to bridge a real cleavage of temperament and outlook; though it does have a part to play in

---

[1] The Bishop of Ely's action in regard to Canon Glazebrook's book *The Faith of a Modern Churchman*, and a petition now being circulated that represents "our Lord's birth from a pure Virgin" and "His bodily Resurrection" as "revealed truths to be constantly held by all faithful Christians . . . as part of a Christian man's duty to GOD", are manifestations of a spirit and an outlook which I believe to be entirely subversive of the outlook and spirit of the Religion of Christ. They are "clothed with the strange trappings and the primitive authority of an age that is altogether alien and hostile to our own" (President Wilson's speech at Washington's grave, July 4, 1918). Indeed, these manifestations are the immediate begetter of this book.

explaining the cause of the cleavage and so, perhaps, in reducing it to its minimum. But I leave this part to others. As regards the claim of these champions of tradition to interpret the Creed in the literal or historical sense of its various articles, it is clear that it could not be maintained before any judicial court of inquiry. They do as we do, only less thoroughly, less consistently : with the result that for them the symmetry and coherence of the Creed is destroyed. One method of interpretation is adopted by them as regards some articles and another method as regards others. The only way in which the original coherence and symmetry of the Creed can be recovered and retained for us all is by full recognition and frank acceptance of the principle that it is to be interpreted both as a whole and in respect of each particular article, neither according to its literal construction, nor according to its legal construction, but according to its religious construction. In the case of each article we are to ask what is the religious conviction, the spiritual reality, to which the literal statement points :— what does it contribute to the affirmation of the whole Christian outlook on the world and human life : what is the 'value' for Religion that Christians have in the past connected with it or deduced from it.

We cannot, indeed, answer this question truly

without reference to the history of the Creed during the times when it was in process of formation. The literal construction of the words, as the 'man in the street' to-day would understand them, does not always give their true sense at the time at which the Creed was formed. It is hardly ever true that an ancient formula 'means just what it says' to a man to-day. Still less, in my judgement, is it true that a man is entitled to profess his faith in the words of the Creed in any sense which he can persuade himself they may bear to-day. In the august Upper House of the Convocation of Canterbury itself not long ago the Bishop of Oxford described as 'ludicrous' a statement on these lines of another distinguished bishop as to the sense in which he understood certain clauses in the Athanasian Creed. And if we are to be loyal to the faith of our Christian forefathers, as expressed in the Creed, we must be at pains to make sure that we know what meanings they attached to its various clauses, what ideas they wished to repudiate, and what were the inward religious truths they intended to safeguard (it was often to safeguard rather than to express) by the form of words they chose. 'Loyalty' is a great word, often, it is to be feared, too lightly used. The will to be loyal is not enough. An exacting intellectual discipline is required of those who claim to be loyal to the early Christian Creed. They must find out what it was; and they cannot do that in a moment. But I know of no nobler aim, no purpose of more abiding worth, than the aim and the purpose to be loyal, in thought as in life, to the spirit of this early Christian Faith. The history of that Faith, in its various manifestations in the world from the earliest times of its origin, has been my own main subject of study and thought for more years than, looking back on their 'results', I care to record. I believe I am familiar with all the evidence and all the arguments that can be used in defence of the traditional conception of the facts. I believe I can state them clearly, and as a teacher by my calling I have been accustomed to put them before the students whose studies I have to guide. I am ready, also, to admit that our modern study, by the method of the 'lower' and the 'higher' criticism, may be mistaken in some of its conclusions, and that the modern champions of the traditional conception may be possessed of those 'highest' critical faculties, and that super-intelligence, which some of them appear to claim in controversy with the 'higher' critics, who have only ordinary intelligence and the capacity for open-minded and painstaking research. There may have been granted to these others an intuitive insight into the complicated problems of the origin and developement of the Christian Religion which the rest of us, who are students of the subject, fail to detect in what they write or say. I cannot hope that any of them will be satisfied with such fruits of my own study as I offer in the following pages. They are offered in the hope that some would-be disciples of Jesus, less serenely and securely established, may be helped by them to be loyal to the Christian Faith, and that a quiet statement of the meaning of the Apostles' Creed according to its religious construction may furnish others with the answer of a good conscience to which they can refer. A good cause, it is said, needs no defence: but it does need to be stated and understood.

I have already endeavoured to make a small contribution towards such a statement, and, as it is by way of a further small contribution that the following pages are intended (I am as conscious as any of my readers can be that I nowhere bring out the meaning in its fulness), it is convenient to recall the facts.

Early in the year 1914 in a published letter to the Bishop of Oxford (*The Miracle of Christianity*: Longmans Green & Co.), which was called forth by a letter of his denouncing 'the critical school' in the Church (*The Times*, December 29, 1913), I urged a plea for the full recognition of a new method of using the ancient Creeds of the Church. *Nove, non nova* was the gist of my plea. I urged that in this difficult matter of interpretation and use of old formularies unity could only be achieved in the Church if attention was concentrated on the religious values of the various articles. I argued that, in the unceasing movement of life, since the Creeds were drawn up, and the always changing environment of knowledge and institutions, only the religious values of the various articles could be constant. And I entreated the Bishop of Oxford for one to welcome into full Christian fellowship with himself, and accept as fellow-workers in the Church and brothers in the ministry, all who could take and use the Creeds according to their religious construction, even though they could not profess belief in all the statements they contain in the literal sense of the words in which their great affirmations of Faith are made. More particularly I begged him to make an early opportunity of "shewing us exactly how the historical happening or phenomenon of the Miraculous Birth (assuming it to be a fact) is related to belief in the Incarnation". Inasmuch as the Bishop of Oxford, in common with most educated members of the Church to-day, does as a matter of fact interpret some of the articles in this way, I hoped that he would admit the reasonableness of the plea that the liberty of interpretation which he allows himself as regards some articles might rightly be extended to others. To my regret, however, the Bishop could only recognize the method as legitimate in the case of the particular articles to which he himself applied it, and he sought to justify the limitation which commended itself to him by distinctions which, again as a matter of fact, have not seemed valid to those of his fellow-Churchmen who thought the wider liberty of interpretation desirable. I venture to add that I do not think they could be convincing to any one who followed the Bishop's frequent appeals to us to really think things out, down to the bottom. Furthermore, to my request that he would enlighten us as to the way in which the manner of our Lord's birth was related to the doctrine of His Person (surely a proper request to any one, whether a bishop or not, who thinks the traditional belief an essential element in the faith of a Christian), no response so far as I am aware has been made. I have therefore myself been obliged to give particular attention to the question, in the form in which it seems to me it can most usefully be considered.

My own letter to the Bishop was followed by a number of pamphlets and statements on the subject by eminent Churchmen. There was also a fairly full discussion in Convocation (April 29 and 30, 1914), after which a declaration was agreed to by the Bishops which upheld, indeed, the traditional beliefs, but sanctioned a large measure of freedom of interpretation for those of the Clergy who felt the

PREFACE

need of it. So, at all events, it was generally understood, when taken in conjunction with the carefully prepared speeches made in the course of the discussion: and recently the Archbishop seems to have confirmed this view of its intention and effect.[1]

The discussion, in and outside Convocation, in any case revealed the fact that the position of the so-called 'critical school', which Dr. Gore denounced, was far too strong to be assailed successfully by the method he adopted, and the body of Churchmen who give it recognition, if not full sympathy, too numerous and too sure of their ground to be browbeaten or silenced.

So it must be admitted, though some Churchmen are loth to admit it, that there are to-day, firmly established in the Church of England, two schools of interpretation of the Creed: and both are there to stay. One of these two schools regards what is called the 'symbolical' interpretation as legitimate in the case of certain articles only, the other is prepared to allow its extension to all.

[1] See the report in *The Guardian* of May 1918 of the proceedings of Convocation (May 2, 1918) in regard to a Petition of the House of Laymen asking the Bishops to take measures to secure that every minister of the Church of England teaches "in conformity with the belief of the Church in regard to our Lord's Nativity". On this occasion the Archbishop, in advising the Bishops to take no fresh action in the matter, referred to the discussion in the Convocation of 1914 as "perhaps the most memorable and careful debate which has for many years been held in this House".

I have written "what is called the 'symbolical' interpretation", because I cannot readily make the phrase my own, and those who use it do not seem to attach to it the same meaning. In our modern parlance the symbol and the thing symbolized by it are not the same, and the symbol is always something of a material or a quasi-material kind. It seems to me an unnatural term to apply either to a verbal statement or to its interpretation.

For example: if our Lord after the Resurrection had a body that was visible, though not susceptible to the law of gravitation except at will; and if in that body He visibly rose from the earth out of sight; then that act of His was, I am sure, not only His passing away from this visible world of ours (as it was), but also a symbol shewing that He had passed into 'the heavenlies'—to use the term we owe to St. Paul. It shewed, and was intended to shew, His disciples that. He had returned to the 'nearer presence' of the invisible Father from whose 'bosom' He came into the world—to the 'glory' which He had with Him from the foundation of the world, or which He had won by His life on earth.[1] The act was a symbol of the spiritual reality that the Church has always intended by 'the Ascension', and I can easily use the clause "He ascended into

[1] Both these points of view are represented in the New Testament; cf. Jn. xvii. 5 and Heb. ii. 9, 10.

heaven, and sitteth on the right hand of the Father" to express that belief. But I cannot speak of the clause, or my interpretation of it, as symbolical. It was the visible act that was symbolical, and the clause at its face value is a simple statement that the act occurred.

Still less can I speak of a symbolical sense of the words when I doubt whether there was any visible act of ascension at all, to be the symbol of anything—when I incline to believe that the whole 'transaction' was one between the Spirit of our Lord and the spirits of a few of His disciples.

But, on the other hand, if I believe that after death He did really enter on a new life, other than life as man in this world, and, with all the enrichment of the human experience through which He had passed, 'return' to the Father of Spirits from whom He had come; then, Copernican in my conception of the universe though I am, I have no difficulty whatever in expressing my belief in the Ptolemaic language of the Creed. It is a terse and picturesque way of saying what I mean. It is, no doubt, a popular way rather than a scientific way: it presents the spiritual reality which I believe in the form of a quasi-physical occurrence. But the clause in its place in the Creed is intended to denote a spiritual valuation of the Person of whom it is affirmed; it is part of the whole appreciation of His significance which the Creed as a whole is intended to express ; and in using its words I intend to make the same affirmation of Faith about Him that the Church has always intended to make. No question of 'science', no physical theory of the universe, comes into my mind at all. I cannot avoid the use of spatial metaphors—some kind of 'movement' seems to 'belong' to every manifestation of life and reality. But the religious conviction I mean to express is what I believe was brought home to the minds and hearts of the earliest disciples of Jesus, and realized and expressed by them, under forms and in terms which were congruous, as such forms and terms always must be, with the intellectual culture of their time.

I may find the whole reality in the Personality of Jesus acting invisibly on their minds and hearts —their personalities—through psychic rather than physical channels. I may believe that the narrative of the Ascension is their interpretation, their rationalization, of a spiritual experience, the basis of which was a spiritual fact. And if I thus share their conviction as to the spiritual fact—not simply the thing that happened at the moment but their valuation of it, the eternal reality itself—I readily accept their mode of stating my own belief. I do not treat their language as symbolical, in the sense that it means or stands for some religious conviction

PREFACE

other than what it seems to state, but as being the expression of a fact about our Lord and the relation in which He is to GOD and to the world and the men whose life He shared.

If I do this, then I am taking the clause of the Creed according to the religious construction of its words. I am assigning to it the meaning which it has in regard to the whole revelation made in the person of Him who was the incarnate Son of GOD.

I am very far from divorcing this meaning from His actual history, or substituting a mere idea for an actual experience of life. Christianity differs from any philosophy in being based on an actual Person, who lived a real life as a man in the world. It is in the impression that our Lord produced and produces that the true history of His life and activity is contained :—the impression He produced on those who knew Him 'in the days of His flesh', and the impression He has produced on millions since : primarily, I suppose, through the accounts which some of His earliest followers gave of their experience ; though it must be remembered that some of the accounts which are most impressive to us probably come from men who had not known Him in those earliest days. Exactly how the impression was produced matters as little to us as the question whether Greek or Aramaic was the ordinary vehicle of His thought and teaching.

If, then, I accept the valuation of that history which the Creed affirms, I am in union with the mind of the Church, whether as the result of study of the evidence I think that the traditional account of each particular incident that is recorded of Him is trustworthy or not.

I have taken the clause on the Ascension as an example almost at hazard. Nearly every clause would afford an equally good illustration of the 'religious construction' of the Creed and the method in which a loyal Churchman may use it to declare his faith. And I chose the title 'The Faith of a Christian' because I desire from the outset to repudiate the thought that such faith as this might more properly be described as only the faith of a 'modern' Christian. It is, I am confident, the faith of a Christian of any and of every age in the troubled history of Christianity in its great past, and in the greater future which awaits it, when the Church, the spirit-bearing body of Christ, become more conscious of the Spirit which is its life, will be the means of diffusing that spirit throughout a world which is already conscious of its need of a life that is Christian.

In view of the special occasion which prompts this attempt at exposition of a point of view which is

PREFACE

still strange to many Christians, I have treated some articles of the Creed at much greater length than others, but I have not attempted more than a sketch that leaves much to be filled in. By way of introduction to the subject as a whole I print for the first time the Prelection which I delivered before the Divinity Faculty of Cambridge (July 19, 1911) before my election as Lady Margaret's Professor. It will be clear, I think, that the interpretation of the Creed which I offer runs on the same lines as the Prelection. And I conclude with a Sermon preached before the University of Cambridge (June 8, 1913), on the conditions of our Lord's life on earth, which is in close relation to the whole issue.

J. F. B.-B.

CAMBRIDGE,
July 7, 1918.

CONTENTS

	PAGE
PREFACE	vii
I. CHRISTIAN DOCTRINE AND THE GOSPELS	1
II. THE UNITY OF THE CREED	29
III. "[I BELIEVE] IN JESUS CHRIST HIS ONLY SON OUR LORD"	41
IV. "WHO WAS CONCEIVED BY THE HOLY GHOST, BORN OF THE VIRGIN MARY"	66
V. "SUFFERED UNDER PONTIUS PILATE, WAS CRUCIFIED, DEAD, AND BURIED, HE DESCENDED INTO HELL"	111
VI. "THE THIRD DAY HE ROSE AGAIN FROM THE DEAD, HE ASCENDED INTO HEAVEN, AND SITTETH ON THE RIGHT HAND OF GOD THE FATHER ALMIGHTY; FROM THENCE HE SHALL COME TO JUDGE THE QUICK AND THE DEAD"	130
VII. "I BELIEVE IN GOD THE FATHER ALMIGHTY, MAKER OF HEAVEN AND EARTH"	140
VIII. "I BELIEVE IN THE HOLY GHOST; THE HOLY CATHOLIC CHURCH; THE COMMUNION OF SAINTS; THE FORGIVENESS OF SINS; THE RESURRECTION OF THE BODY, AND THE LIFE EVERLASTING"	152
IX. READJUSTMENT	179
X. THE CROSS THE SYMBOL OF THE INCARNATION	197

I

CHRISTIAN DOCTRINE AND THE GOSPELS

WHEN I was required to choose a title for this prelection without delay, I simply put side by side together the two subjects of study which for many years past have been constantly before me :—subjects of study that has been fascinating and absorbing, but also (I need not shrink from saying it) often anxious and perplexed.

And if, in treating of it now, I adopt the more personal rather than the purely abstract manner, it is for this reason. In this as in all studies I would fain make my own the motto in which Augustine summed up his estimate of Cyprian's conception of the Church as a great society of those who without detriment to their sense of common fellowship in aim, communion of faith and allegiance, could take and allow in others various points of view : *Saluo iure communionis, diuersa sentire.*

There are so many different points of view in the New Testament itself. It is only, I believe, by allowing these their full force that we can come again to realize the true significance and nature of that deep underlying harmony—the very name of which has disappeared even from the title-page of our students' text-books on the Gospels.

The question which I propose to deal with is this: How is Christian Doctrine affected by the methods of study of the Gospels, the knowledge, or the theories as to the processes by which they were composed, which particularly during the last ten years have been winning more and more acceptance among English students and have become more widely known to the public at large?

Some of these methods and some of these theories are startlingly new. Some of them seem to me to fit in so naturally to much of the most stimulating teaching of one of the most stimulating teachers I was allowed to hear in my early days in Cambridge, that though the voice and the accent is often very different, I cannot feel that the spirit is alien. The symbolism of miracles, the spiritual significance of the Fourth Gospel; the use of every kind of knowledge available to arrive at the exact words used, the exact sense of the words to the mind of the speaker and to the minds of those he addressed; and then, no literal transference of them to other conditions and times and minds, but a 'proportionate interpretation'. These are the lines on which much of the most fruitful recent investigation has proceeded, and many a long composite German phrase simply connotes enquiries of this kind. *Fas est et ab hoste doceri*—if indeed 'hostis' he be.

I think that the critical study of the Gospels has done the chief part of its work, so far at least as it is likely to affect either the contents or the exposition of Christian Doctrine; and that, accordingly, it is possible already to estimate its contribution in this respect.

But so many of what are claimed as assured results are only in my judgement well-based working-hypotheses, and there is still so much uncertainty, that it is only a 'point of view' that any one can offer.

I would approach the question as one who is convinced that what is called the modern method of study of the Gospels is not only inevitable but in itself desirable, and that many of the results to which it is leading us, however embarrassing at the moment, will surely throw fresh light for us on the Mind of GOD, on the way in which He was pleased that the crowning revelation of His purpose towards us should be *made*, and then *transmitted* to the generations of men to come.

I would approach the question as one who is convinced that the author of the Fourth Gospel truly interpreted his Master's meaning when he represented Him, in speaking to His disciples—surely not only of the earlier but also of the later times as well—as bidding them expect no absolute and final intellectual illumination which would leave them nothing else to learn, but rather patiently await the results of the quiet process by which His Spirit, which was also His Father's Spirit, would shew them the way, would gradually guide them, by the use of all their own faculties, through all their own experiences of life—and lead them stage by stage :—'no end to learning'. Enough if stage by stage they could learn, individually *and* as a body, by this never-ending process, the truth for them at the moment; seeking to do the will of GOD, they should come to know the doctrine.

The full correlation of these successive experiences would never perhaps be consciously achieved. But it is of course to such attempts at the correlation of experience among the earliest Christians that under GOD'S providence we owe our New Testament and in later times our whole scheme of Christian Doctrine with all its variations in expression and detail from time to time, the particular appreciation of it in every age inherently and inevitably responsive to the intellectual or moral or social or even political conditions of the time—now expansive, adventurous, full of hope and vigour, and now for a season more rigid, less supple, less vital, less receptive of new methods and new ideas.

We owe the books of our New Testament to a few writers who were specially qualified, by knowledge or experience or opportunities of research, to attempt from different points of view to record and interpret the facts, to meet actual needs of the moment, in relation to past and current conceptions and expectations. That in doing this they were enabled to meet needs of a distant future, which they could never have anticipated, is one of the surest proofs of their 'inspiration'. And ability to meet the needs of ordinary Christian men and women is the test by which any fresh attempts to interpret the experience of the past in relation to the knowledge and conceptions of a later age must be judged. But these attempts have always come from those who are relatively few :—the students and teachers who have time to think and who learn while they teach, who are always ready to readjust themselves, who are in fact with more or less constant intention doing so all their lives.

I do not believe that any interpretation of the present can be true that does not include and account for the faith of the Church of the past.

It is such a body of students and teachers—the divinity faculty of Cambridge—many of them in one way or other my own teachers, to whom I have to address to-day, as a fellow-student, a short and tentative survey of a subject which whole courses of lectures would not exhaust.

And as it is only such a body that I am required to address, I may merely allude to things which would need explanation at length to others who were less familiar with the subject.

I will try at the outset to make my point of view of it clear.

I cannot share the light-heartedness, the gaiety, of those who seem to approach the study of the Gospels as a merely literary problem and sometimes give utterance to their opinions with a kind of 'fine careless rapture' that is more stimulating than convincing. But I do believe that to some of them we owe pioneer work of the highest value, the opening-out of paths by which we can march forward— προκοπὴ τοῦ εὐαγγελίου. The literary problem is there. The critics do not make it. For the solution of it a certain detachment of mind, a certain unperturbed aloofness even from most cherished convictions, is probably needed. And on the correct solution of the problem depends a true conception of the inspiration of the books.

CHRISTIAN DOCTRINE

Nor again can I share altogether the optimistic views of some of those who are sure that the Gospels will emerge unscathed from the most searching criticism that can be applied to them. I think we have *something* to fear: and yet, that what we have to fear is only what every age has had to fear when there is happening the removal of things that can be shaken, which have long been regarded as the permanently abiding things that cannot be shaken. Those who are peculiarly the guardians of our great religious tradition, and are themselves rich in Christian experience and conviction, may well be confident that Christianity itself will remain in all its strength. They may well be confident that the Gospel will be prized and treasured as highly in the future as ever in the past. That confidence I share. *But* I think it is certain that the authority of the Gospels will be of a different *kind*. And it is just this question of their authority—living authority to-day—that raises the investigation above the sphere of merely literary or antiquarian interest.

I can only take one or two representative examples which must include theories about the Messiahship and the narratives of miracles and the Resurrection.

I leave on one side theories which have nothing

to do with the literary criticism of the Gospels in relation to Christian Doctrine, though some of them need to be examined carefully in connexion with the credibility of particular narratives or the evidences of Christianity in general; and some of them derive support from the methods followed and the conclusions reached by a certain class of literary critics.

I would take first the theory, almost universally accepted, that the records of our Lord's life and teaching are to some extent coloured by later experience and reflexion. This is a theory which seems to me to be so firmly based as to be irresistible. Of course it is not altogether new. As regards the Fourth Gospel at least it was partly recognized in our own great classic commentary, more than thirty years ago, and though the principle has been extended far more widely since, I do not think that Christian Doctrine is much affected by wider acceptance of the principle. So far as we can trace modifications of the original tradition in St. Matthew or St. Luke, and have good reasons for suspecting them even in St. Mark, we simply put back by a few years particular developements of interpretation. Most of us have already—independently of any recent literary criticism—ceased to base important doctrines on isolated sayings or phrases or details in illustrative parables of our Lord. We believe that He Himself is the essential Christian revelation—the Way, the Truth, and the Life, and that if those wonderful words were never spoken *by* Him, they are none the less true *of* Him. If it is the case in regard to some of the traditional 'proof-texts' of doctrine that we cannot claim them with the same certitude as of old as coming to us with our Lord's own authority, in His very own words: if we have to recognize a larger element of reflective interpretation of later experience on the part of the various writers, or in the sources from which they drew; our acceptance of the doctrine taught or implied need not be the less whole-hearted.

If, during our Lord's visible ministry on earth in human form, His consciousness of His unique relation to GOD the Father was less constant and continuous than St. John, for example, represents it; if His knowledge of many things was as limited as some suppose, and as He is depicted as declaring it to be in at least one particular—well, let me use the simplest words. It all brings our Lord much closer to us, He in His course on earth to us men in ours. It makes more real to us some of the phrases of the Epistle to the Hebrews—that most human of all the books of our New Testament. And if St. Mark, and even St. Matthew, did not shrink from perpetuating the tradition that our Lord's last and only words from the Cross were the despairing cry " My GOD, my GOD, why hast thou forsaken me ? "— we with nineteen centuries behind us of experience of His power, risen and ascended, need not shrink from recognition of the fact, if fact it be, that the veiling of His divine consciousness, the limitations of His knowledge and power, during His visible ministry on earth were much more real than the ordinary reader of our Gospels would suppose:—though it is the writers of the Gospels themselves who give us the means of judging.

We speak of our Lord's 'accommodating' his teaching to the knowledge and ideas of the time: and in a measure no doubt we are justified in doing so. The master-builders and sculptors of Greece knew and practised the *entasis* of the column, that it might produce the effect of straightness at the distance they desired: and the Master Teacher of spiritual things may well have practised a kind of intellectual and spiritual *entasis*. The teacher of any subject must adapt his language and illustrations, and to some extent the range of his ideas, to the capacities of his pupils.

But I can find nothing inconsistent with the doctrine of the Incarnation in the view that our Lord "in the days of his flesh . . . while he learnt obedience from the things which he suffered", was limited in His conscious knowledge of things literary, historical, and scientific, to the ordinary knowledge and ideas current among the people to whom He came, while the evidence the Gospels give us of mental conflict and struggle, of very human anxiety and uncertainty as to which way the Divine Will pointed Him at crises, and as to the actual part he was to play in the fulfilment of GOD'S purposes :— this evidence is far too strong ever to have been ignored, though it has only an ambiguous place in formal doctrine and remains in the Gospels a mystery—a mystery the secret of which, however, is sometimes partly learnt by those who have been in 'the deep waters' of suffering and doubt and perplexity themselves, or have had to try to bring consolation and strength to others who are passing through them. These very 'limitations', as we call them, of the earthly life immensely increase the spiritual force of the appeal of the Christ.

For the rest, every Churchman who—I must not say 'uses' but—'understands' the words of the Athanasian Creed knows that the full and complete manhood of our Lord is as integral a part of the doctrine of the Incarnation as His Godhead; and no member of the Church of England at all events is committed to any definition of authority which precludes him from considering, and it may be accepting, the hypotheses I have mentioned. Students of technical 'authoritative' doctrine know the term κένωσις. The term itself, though derived, I believe, from a mistaken interpretation of a phrase of St. Paul's, expresses a doctrine necessary to the scientific theologian; but there has always been uncertainty among theologians in their attempts to apply it. It recognizes a series of facts about our Lord's life, the implications of which have not found detailed expression in Christian theology. It safeguards the doctrine of the Incarnation; but it does not define the extent of the limitation of the Divine Son of GOD—temporary and voluntary—which was involved in the assumption of real manhood in a real human life lived in the world at a definite epoch in its history.

These instances of the relation between the results of modern critical study of the Gospels and Christian Doctrine as a whole—though they cause perplexity and uneasiness to some—are perhaps too obvious or too general to be offered to the notice of those to whom I am speaking now.

Let me take one particular theory which, when it was first propounded, seemed to me to be more subversive of traditional Christian conceptions than any other theory which I could regard as a legitimate inference from the evidence of the Gospels and Jewish thought of the time, so far as this Jewish thought of the time is really known apart from the Gospels: a theory which if it was true seemed likely more than others to call for reconstruction of some of the 'proofs' of Christian Doctrine.

This theory brought before us two series of startling questions. The first series begins with the question, Did Jesus ever claim to be the Messiah at all? Then, if He was conscious of being the Messiah, did He not keep this consciousness as a secret from all but a few of His most trusted disciples? Was not this the very secret that Judas betrayed, and so brought on the catastrophe?

This first series of questions need not delay us long.

That our Lord did deem Himself to be the Messiah is recognized as certain even by many of those who tend to believe that in these matters whatever else is right 'tradition' must be wrong. If, as He grew in wisdom and in stature, our Lord grew too in His human consciousness in this respect, and if the knowledge that He regarded Himself as destined to fulfil the Messiah's part was much less widely extended than the narratives imply; if His disciples' later vivid belief in His Messiahship has influenced some of those narratives; no Christian doctrine is affected. Indeed I would go farther and express my own conviction that even if He had never made or allowed this claim, if the

Resurrection was needed before His disciples could make it for Him, they were right—divinely guided—to see in Him the fulfilment of all the prophetic aspirations of the past, the heir of all the partial and manifold revelations of GOD'S own people, the realization of 'the hope of Israel'.

But there is a second series of questions that are put to us.

Accepting the fact that He claimed and avowed the claim to be the Messiah, in what sense did He deem Himself to be Messiah? Was it not only in the sense that He was the Person destined to introduce at some unknown time in the future, after suffering and rejection by His people, the supernatural order of things which the Kingdom of GOD and the rule of His Saints implied: so that He was already the Messiah-to-be, and the powers of the kingdom were already working — though as yet but partially—through Him? And if this be so, was not His ethical teaching conditioned by this conception and only intended to apply to the interval between His death and His subsequent coming back in glory?

These are questions that need more mature consideration than they have yet received, before they can be fully answered. But they have been before us some time; they have been before all younger students of the Gospel history in this home of things new and old; and I do not think it is premature to anticipate affirmative answers to them at least so far as to indicate how affirmative answers to them would not be incompatible with traditional Christian Doctrines.

I take the last question first, because it has least to do with the subject and is receptive of an answer less indefinite and incomplete. No one, I believe, has ever professed belief in Christian Doctrine simply on the evidence of the ethical teaching of our Lord. Many, indeed, have accepted this teaching as of quasi-divine authority who have rejected the Church's belief in the Incarnation. Even if this teaching was intended to apply to the interim only, before the manifestation of the transcendent Christ and the complete establishment of the kingdom; if it was only meant to express the principles of conduct here and now, the spirit, which would fit men for membership of the kingdom when it came:—that is just what Christians have always believed. We are still living in that interim. The doctrine of the Ascension teaches that the Christ already reigns in Heaven, or from Heaven, not that He already reigns on earth with undivided sway. We still pray daily that the kingdom may come—come as it never yet has come on earth: that the will of GOD, frustrated in our experience as it has been and is, may be done here in earth as it is in heaven. We know it is not done yet, and that even when we have the purpose, we often have not the power, to make the principles we accept operative in the conditions in which we live. The conception of an *Interims-Ethik* is not really new to Christians. It may indeed serve to quicken an essentially Christian belief.

And again, we are to-day so much under the domination of evolutionary hypotheses that we tend to forget the fact that *not all* progress and developement is gradual and calm. We need to remind ourselves that violent upheaval and volcanic change —destruction of the existing order before the work of quiet reconstruction can begin—are written on the face of the universe, in the history of peoples, and in the secret chronicles of many a human soul.

Nor do I think that the other conceptions newly put before us are irreconcileable with the Church's belief that the kingdom of the Christ in its fulness is still to-be ; with the earnest expectation of the first generations of Christians, who only slowly came to realize the meaning of some of our Lord's sayings on the subject ; or with the parables of slow, unseen, incalculable progress, through ordinary means and ordinary human effort in the world as it is :—parables which I believe are certainly as integral a part of our Lord's teaching as any of the parables or sayings which seem to reflect more directly the conceptions of one who looked for a sudden catastrophe and change of the existing order of the world, through purely superhuman agencies.

Nor can we ignore the early faith of the Church that it was only by and after the Resurrection that Jesus was proved to be the Christ, entered into His glory, and became possessed of powers that, though in a sense they were already His before, yet were not entirely at His disposal before.

These new conceptions are not irreconcileable with these old beliefs; and they make intelligible some of the sayings, inimitably genuine, to which little definite meaning has hitherto been attached.

I would single out one of these sayings which has only lately received, I believe, its true interpretation in the light of the new hypotheses. It is the saying, "I have a baptism to be baptized with; and how am I straitened till it be accomplished." Πῶς συνέχομαι; How am I constrained, hindered, hemmed in, 'limited'! This strange exclamation is not unnatural from one who was conscious of powers that could not yet expand till the baptism of death released Him from the restraints of His present condition.

"How am I straitened!" We have our Lord's own authority for the view that the limitations of His life on earth were such that He could not be altogether Himself while He was here as Man. And any attempt to base an explanation of our Lord's Person solely on the 'facts' of His life on earth ending in the catastrophe of the Cross is doomed to failure. It is not enough to know Christ 'after the flesh', simply as He was to those that knew Him then. And whether St. Paul (as some maintain)—whether St. Paul knew Him in this way or not, or simply knew what are called the 'facts' about His life, he knew that these facts did not supply the basis for an adequate faith in His Person; and though he had known Christ 'after the flesh', he refused to know Him so any longer.

I proceed to the narratives of the Resurrection. But I cannot pass over in silence the narratives of miracles in general.

With regard to these I have no desire to add a paradox to the many epigrams that are current, whether they come from a sceptical philosopher and historian of the eighteenth century, a man of letters and poet of the nineteenth, who made theology his hobby, or a scholar and divine of the twentieth expressing himself in the honoured terms of the textual critic.

But I must avow my conviction that, so far as the presentation of Christian Doctrine to this generation is concerned, the question whether our Lord actually wrought such miracles, or not, is

one that might well be allowed a little rest. And
I suppose it is some dim recognition of this
fact that leads many earnest disciples to-day to
seek out diligently—and others to acquiesce in—
'natural' explanations of as many as possible of
the miracles recorded in the Gospels: although
these 'natural' explanations not only rob the
miracles of all the evidential value they had, and
still have, to people less affected by naturalistic
theories of the universe, but also—a much more serious
loss—rob the *narratives* of them of their permanent
worth for the true interpretation of the Person of
our Lord. For they are, as they stand, an unparalleled revelation of an unparalleled Personality.

I need scarcely say, even in passing, that no
kind of literary criticism can eliminate these narratives
from the Gospel history, though it can point to a few
which are so different in character from the rest as
to suggest some misunderstanding or the use of less
trustworthy traditions by the particular evangelist in
regard to them. Nor shall I argue against the assumption that a later writer could not have had better
information than an earlier writer as to important
events and determining motives even at chief crises
in the great drama he depicts, or again the assumption
that seems to me equally unwarranted that a
particular writer could not have omitted to record
some one particular miracle—even of highest im-

portance—if he had heard of it. Nor need I dwell at the moment on the fact that many of the conceptions of the nature of our 'material' environment which have unavoidably influenced students of the *origines* of Christianity in the past are now giving place to others that do not seem to justify the *praejudicium* which has prevailed against the narratives of miracles in the Gospels.

I need not dwell on these considerations. But I do desire to emphasize my conviction that Christian Doctrine knows and needs but one use only of the narratives to-day. *They witness to the impression which our Lord actually produced.* That is solid fact, unshakeable history.

Whether we shall ever get nearer than we are to an explanation of the physical or psychological conditions in or by which the effect was produced,—this is a question with which we are not concerned. Browning's treatment of it in *A Death in the Desert* has not yet, I believe, been superseded. It is a matter of little moment too whether, had we been present, 'we' should have given exactly the same account or not. I adopt another's words here, only to add that the specialists and the religious leaders of the time did not give exactly the same account of them then, and I fear very few of 'us' would have given nearly as good an account. And that would matter much.

For if it is rather to other parts of the Gospel history that we must look for evidence of the actual teaching and the inner consciousness of our Lord, so far as we are allowed to know it, in His earthly life, it is to the narratives of the miracles chiefly that we owe our knowledge of the impression He actually produced on ordinary simple folk. Without these narratives the student of Christian Doctrine—the subject of whose study in all its amazing ramifications is yet always the Person of our Lord—the student of Christian Doctrine as well as the apologist of Christianity would be immeasurably the poorer in the materials for his task. It is only the close student of the narratives of the miracles to whom is disclosed, in all its strength and grace, in all its human sympathy and superhuman power, the full significance of the Person of whom such traditions could be told : — traditions instinct with actual experience of His insight into the needs of the men among whom He moved and of His power to satisfy those needs. That, I venture to think, is the kind of history we want : something that lets us see what those who knew Him really felt about Him.

What character, what personality, do these narratives reveal? This is the only note of interrogation which as a student of Doctrine I would affix to them, and that not surreptitiously in the margin and in a bracket, but in the largest type in the text itself.

It is the Venerable Bede, whom Cambridge used to claim as her own, who tells us in his preface that "the true law of history" is the single-minded transmission of current belief.

Judged by this test the narratives of miracles in the Gospels stand firm as faithful records of experience. And their historical value would remain—and in some measure be enhanced—even if some current theories as to the character of the Fourth Gospel were more securely based than they are. For *if* the writer deliberately framed new narratives of miracles (apparently as simple and direct as any in the earlier Gospels) to be the vehicle of his own theological interpretation of the Christ, it could only be because he knew that similar narratives were current as part of the earliest tradition, and because he recognized the value of their evidence for the purpose which he had in view—that purpose of winning men to "believe that Jesus was the Christ, the Son of GOD". They were the 'signs' of the Son of GOD.

For the writer of the Fourth Gospel the appearances of the Risen Lord were among these 'signs' of One who not only 'was raised' but, as our Creed says, 'rose' again:—the two terms struggle for mastery in some important passages in our manuscripts: One who 'rose' by the inherent power of His own Person. And though I propose to speak of them from this point of view, it is not because I suppose that the fact of the Resurrection itself has been in any way impaired by the kind of literary criticism that I have in view throughout. I could not be here to-day if I did. For the Resurrection, with its corollary or sequel the Ascension, is really the one central proof of the Divine Mission, and therefore of the Divine authority of Jesus of Nazareth. It was so regarded by the first preachers of the new faith, who ascribe it to the immediate agency of GOD. It was seeing the risen and ascended Christ that convinced St. Paul. It was the certitude which this vision gave him—a vision as real to him as any of the appearances of the Lord he chronicles —that was to St. Paul the mainspring of all his faith in Him.

We cannot assume that St. Paul knew the words which St. Matthew in characteristic phraseology records of the risen Lord :—" Lo, I am with you all the days, to the consummation of the age " ; or the Johannine teaching of the continuous process of the coming of the ascended Christ or His Spirit to His disciples. We cannot, I say, assume this. But at least his whole conception of being 'in Christ' is instinct with the same spiritual experience, some supreme experience of the soul which underlies the representation of facts in the Gospels. With the conviction which this brought him, and with this conviction alone, he had a Gospel to preach. It is primary and central. Without it, for all of us, the doctrine of atonement, the whole doctrine of the Incarnation, has no really solid basis to rest on. The believer may well bow his head when he recites the mysteries of the Incarnation and the Passion— "came down, was incarnate . . ., suffered, crucified, for us men and for our salvation". He can raise it again when he comes to the Resurrection and Ascension.

As to the narratives of the appearances of the risen Lord, we must recognize the fact that if the New Testament evidence, including of necessity St. Paul's, is more full than the evidence for any other experience recorded in its pages, it is also at the same time more varied and more complicated. We may find ourselves unable to co-ordinate and harmonize it in detail. We may believe that there are different points of view expressed, that some of the narratives are based on surer insight into the actual conditions of the experience than others. But I deprecate any attempt at summary statements of conclusions in such a matter, apart from all the details of the evidence; and I am much more concerned to say that none of these beliefs or suppositions, and no psychological speculations with which I am acquainted, shake the conviction that in these narratives we are face to face with a genuine experience of real men and women, singly, in twos and threes, in companies, in crowds. And belief in the reality of the cause is an inevitable corollary to this conviction. One and the same living Person whom they had known making Himself known to them yet again and afresh, in the new conditions of His life: the knowledge coming to them as only they were able to receive it, in terms of their mental and spiritual constitution.

They are narratives that read like the simplest transcript of personal experience :—that is their 'face value'. And the fact of this experience remains the solid basis of Christian doctrine—the experience of those who were nearest to the facts, who actually lived through those days of shock, those days of despair succeeded by conviction that He who was dead was alive again, ready at the moment ordained in the counsels of GOD to be manifested in His full power and nature, and meanwhile able to inspire His followers with strength to face the interval, with fresh insight into His will and purposes and the certainty that these would prevail, and that all things would work together for good to them that love the GOD He revealed and seek to do His will.

"The voice of the Lord GOD walking in the garden in the cool of the day" was heard by Adam and Eve, and in the fulness of the times in the twilight of daybreak or of evening He again made His voice audible through His Son to those that could hear. He made Himself visible to those that could see. If belief in 'the empty tomb' is necessary to this belief, literary criticism of the narratives does not shake such evidence of that belief as they furnish. Yet the other narratives seem to indicate that it was not the empty tomb that produced the conviction, but rather the personal experience that is expressed in terms of seeing and hearing.

I can only add a few words of summary and retrospect.

I have presented a point of view—as regards the bases of Christian Doctrine the point of view from which I have for many years studied and taught the subject, and I believe this point of view has been well tested and is more widely accepted now than it was some years ago: Christian Doctrine the interpretation of actual experience—experience of our Lord Himself when He lived on earth as man and of those who lived with Him through that life and its unparalleled sequel (that is the firm historical basis); but also the experience of later generations too (this is surely 'historical' also): so that interpretation is always of the present as well as of the past, instant, immediate—as the realization of Christian experience is ever being renewed. It is as the records of such experience in the earliest times of which we have knowledge of it that we value and study the Gospels and other books of our New Testament.

I have tried to bring some of the hypotheses, which seem to me to be well based, with regard to the narratives of the Gospels, into relation to this point of view, and to suggest that such reconstruction of traditional readings of the course of events in the life of our Lord as they involve does not necessarily conflict with traditional Christian Doctrine, and even in some particulars may illumine it and strengthen its foundations, for us in our generation.

Without a solid basis in fact, the doctrine of the Incarnation—the Christian interpretation of life— might remain indeed the grandest philosophy of life that has ever been conceived, the quintessence of the highest moral and spiritual thought of the children of earth: a philosophy which by its intrinsic power of attraction would draw to itself the loyalty of many a human life. There might always be some who without religious conviction would live "as seeing the invisible", and by happy experience of earthly love and goodness and beauty would brace themselves to believe that the awful pain and evil and waste and ugliness in the world as it is were not the appalling and final realities they sometimes seem to be:—nay, rather that there is in and behind it all a purpose, a will, of Good—powerful as well as loving—that is being worked out, that can turn to good even here and now much of the pain and the evil, and some day will be realized fully. But a philosophy such as this is not for ordinary men and women, who need a *religion*. And the doctrine of the Incarnation is only a religion if it has a firm historical foundation in the ascertainable facts of our Lord's life and teaching. Only then if it is based on fact—fact, past and present—does the dream, the vision, become reality for ordinary human beings—the vital truth for them as they are in the world as it is, by which they can live, content to

wait
Death—nor be afraid.

II

THE UNITY OF THE CREED

IT is often said that the Apostles' Creed is little more than a summary of the main facts about our Lord's life in the world and the effects it produced. The meaning of its statements is plain. We must either take them or leave them, just as they are. It is, indeed, true that our Creeds are rather dull things: there is nothing of the passion of faith about them. The Apostles' Creed in particular, on the face of it, is a singularly undemonstrative document: it suggests little of the warmth and glow of the Christian's appreciation of life — his attitude to it and his estimate of its possibilities and purpose. Its 'face' value is clearly not its real value. But no Creed can ever be understood when regarded as a document by itself. It cannot say all it means: ecclesiastical formulas never do. Though the primary purpose of Creeds was for use in baptism, in enrolling new members of the

Church, they never expressed the whole faith of the Church; and their growth and expansion was due to controversies: the additions made from time to time being designed to defend against other views what was believed to be inherent in the tradition of the Church. They need to be supplemented always by this, for the most part inarticulate, unwritten tradition, the living feeling and practice and worship of the Church, which are outside their range. It is only against this background, and in this environment, that they can be seen in their right perspective and true proportions. Apart from it they stand out too sharply. The experience out of which they grew was essentially ethical and spiritual; and for the expression of ethical and spiritual experience such formulas can never be a satisfactory medium. It is in life and worship, in thought and aspiration, that experience of this kind is realized; its spirit cannot be confined in definitions; and we may learn more of the real faith of members of the Church at any given time from knowledge of what they were doing, how they were living and praying, how they were meeting the special difficulties and dangers and problems that confronted them, than we can learn from their formal statements of belief. For example, we should fare ill if we had a Creed of St. Paul instead of his letters and notes of his work; and

THE UNITY OF THE CREED

the human documents which have survived of the early centuries of the Church's life, letters, inscriptions over tombs, sermons, prayers, biographies and martyrdoms, are of much more value than would be the Creeds of the persons concerned or of the Churches of which they were members. How did they really face life and death?

We know almost nothing about the 'Creed' of Antioch at the beginning of the second century. We cannot reconstruct it, if there was one. But the seven letters of its bishop, Ignatius, written as he travelled a prisoner in chains to martyrdom at Rome, reveal to us what no 'Creed' could have revealed of the faith of the man himself and of the teaching a bishop gave, of whom but for the chance of his martyrdom no record would have come to us. We need not mind what the 'Creed' of the Church of Antioch was. We know what we need to know about it, if we read the letters of Ignatius.[1] It is only historical study that shows these things and so supplies the background and atmosphere of formulas. The real meaning of the Apostles' Creed is not as plain as it seems to be.

[1] These letters can be read in English in the excellent edition by Dr. Srawley in the series 'Early Church Classics' published by the S.P.C.K. Such a biography as Gregory of Nyssa's *Life of St. Macrina* in the same series (by Mr. W. K. L. Clarke) is another example of the kind of intimate history that we need if we are to understand the faith of a Christian nearly three centuries later.

Again, not seldom, it is asserted that the statements in the Apostles' Creed are statements of historical facts or events as well attested as any other facts or events in human history, and that we may be said to know them as well as we know any events of the past. Yet this assertion, even as regards the clauses of the Creed to which it could truly apply at all, has nothing to do with the true interpretation or use of a Creed. The purpose of a Creed is not to profess knowledge, but to declare faith. Faith is on a different plane from knowledge; and the intention of the Creed is not to state historical 'facts', or events, but the religious convictions of the Society and the individual who makes the convictions of the Society his own.[1] The exact meaning attached to the various

[1] I agree with scarcely anything that Professor Sidgwick years ago wrote on the question of the legitimate use of ancient Creeds, but I do agree that the use of the Creeds in the Church of England implies an individual profession of faith and not merely a general assent to a collective expression of the teaching of the Church. Nor, for my own part, could I be happy in using a Creed unless I was satisfied that, with regard to each part of the Creed, I believed the substance of what the Church had intended by it in the past—unless, indeed, as is the case with the 'damnatory clauses' of the Athanasian Creed, every one concerned knew that we did not believe to-day what the framers of the Creed did believe and plainly said. Yet the Creeds we have inherited are so ill fitted for the purpose of expressing clearly the essential convictions (whether intellectual, moral, or spiritual) of a Christian, that the use of them in public worship is one of the reasons why some of those who are most Christian in mind and will are not to be found in our churches at all. In these circumstances the Creeds cannot retain the authority which is often claimed for them.

clauses of the Creed by the Church as a whole has varied a good deal at different times, and individuals who did not fall into line with the interpretation prevailing at the moment have always been suspect. It has never been belief in the mere 'fact' that counted as the individual's faith, guaranteeing him the fellowship of the Church on earth and in heaven, but always the meaning which it had for him, the inferences he drew from it, the opinions connected with it which he held or was supposed to hold. Many of these opinions and inferences have come and gone with the rise and fall of political and social institutions, or with changes in men's general outlook on the universe and life. Yet many of them have affected the thought and practice of the Church so profoundly that they have lingered on, long past their time, after they have ceased to have the real relation to contemporary thought and life they had at first. They held the field once undisputed, and they survive by the force of habit and the wonderful power of possession, outliving the time when they contribute anything useful to the elucidation of the living faith of a living Church.

So it is not easy to say what has been the constant or permanent element in the faith of the Church as regards a particular clause of its Creed. Yet the attempt is worth making. The Apostles'

Creed has been fixed and unchanged for more than a thousand years, indeed in effect for more than half as long again,—though not, as Christians believed for most of that time, the actual composition clause by clause of the twelve Apostles themselves. Our other Creeds are even older than the Apostles' Creed in its final form. Of all the amazing developements of human activities and interests since that time—of all the changes in men's conceptions of history, philosophy, and science—not one has left a trace on the Creeds. It is not that the Church has stood still: it has lived a full, if not a full enough, life in this changing world. Yet as regards the Creed the only change or developement it has admitted has been a change or developement in the interpretation of some of its clauses. Quietly and almost unconsciously it has grown out of the case, as it were, in which its faith was contained, and slipped it off. The phenomenal, or 'factual', cover of the belief has worn out, and a process of re-interpretation has ensued. In this process we have throughout maintained fidelity to the religious conception that was expressed in words that are no longer literally true to us. It might be said that we go on using the old words in new senses. But this is only true to a very limited extent, and the change that has taken place goes deeper than words: it affects the meaning of whole clauses.

Yet, on the other hand, further reflexion leads us to the conviction that the fundamental sense is not new. It is what has always been the 'religious' sense of the article in question. And the result of the process, however it should be described, is to bring out more clearly the spiritual values and the ethical bearings of the old belief. To borrow Dr. Sanday's phrase, "the total force of the central truth" of each such article has not been impaired.

Yet as regards the Creed of the Church as a whole something has undoubtedly been lost. For the process of re-interpretation has been consciously applied only to some of its clauses. We have taken account of the change in our outlook only here and there, as regards this or that clause, which we were fain to think lay not at the centre but only at the circumference of our main beliefs. And some have done so in respect of one clause and others in respect of another. So that the unity of the Creed has been destroyed, and we are now at sixes and sevens as regards its use. We want a new perspective in which to see it as a whole.

It is well for us to be warned against 'clipping the faith', and to be told how important 'perspective' is in these matters:—" If you take a really great work of art, you cannot separate any part of the picture without damage to the whole."[1] We may welcome the words: they are surely true of that 'really great work of art', the Creed of the Church. Though it grew and grew in its actual formation, yet it is as a finished product the work of times when Reason was the handmaid of Religion. It was fashioned into form by men possessed of all the learning of their age, who had carefully thought out the *rationale* of the traditional beliefs and institutions of the Church, and expressed them in relation to their whole scheme of things and to one another. It is all on the same plane of thought— or, to keep the metaphor of the picture, the tone and colour and treatment are all one, every part of the picture is intimately related to every other part in due subordination to the central figure—" Jesus Christ [GOD'S] only Son, our Lord, conceived by the Holy Ghost, born of the Virgin Mary . . . very GOD of very GOD . . . came down from heaven . . . rose again from the dead . . . descended into hell . . . ascended into heaven . . . will come again in glory." The coherence of the various clauses of the Creed is perfect.

The point is this. The central conception of the Creed, as a work of art, to which everything else in it conforms, is that of the world as the centre of

[1] The Bishop of Winchester—speech in Convocation, April 29-30, 1914 (*The Guardian*, May 7, 1914).

the universe, with GOD outside it, up in heaven, intervening miraculously in its affairs. He made the world by His *fiat*. There is an order of Nature, and its whole order is in a sense the expression of His will and under His control: but at any moment He can intervene and change it. He does so whenever He pleases to manifest Himself. His manifestation of Himself in the Person of His Son was attended by many such signs of superhuman and supernatural character, wrought in and on the order of Nature—voices, or merely peals of thunder, according as men could hear or interpret them; dazzling lights by which theophanies were regularly accompanied.

So too in the Creed the Gospels are all alike accepted as literal history. Our Lord's Body is a human body of the substance of His Mother, but in it He can walk on water.

The whole course of His life, His coming into the world and His leaving it, are marked by 'miracles'. A revelation wrought out in the world of sense by a historical Person who entered the world by a miracle was attended all through by outward miraculous manifestations.

Hell is a place under the earth to which He went down. He will visibly come again with glorious accompaniments to hold a great Assize. The same supernatural power which He had over

His own Body will be manifested in the restoration of the bodies of all men at this last Assize. The miraculous powers over Nature which He had were leased by Him in some measure to the Church He founded.

All the articles of the Creed are in keeping with these general conceptions. The Creed is a unity as long as they hold good. But as regards many of the articles they have ceased to hold good for us. There has been a great growth of knowledge outside the Creed. We use many of the old words in new senses; and by our patchwork re-interpretation we have destroyed the coherence of the whole.

The case is almost exactly the same as regards the more philosophical statements of the faith of the Church which we have inherited. Like the Apostles' Creed, they register the thought of their period; they are perfectly coherent in their original framework of historical, philosophical, and scientific presuppositions. They come to us in the fashion of their time. The categories of thought in which they are expressed are not ours to-day. The questions with which they are concerned do not present themselves to us in the same form. They are not looked at by us from the same angle of vision. When they are still, as many of them are, 'live' questions, they have to be—if the metaphor from Art may be

THE UNITY OF THE CREED

kept—'posed' by us in an entirely different way.[1] Between our modes of thought and our theological formulas there is not the correspondence and congruity that is necessary if the formulas are really to be the expression of ourselves. This, no doubt, is the explanation of the fact that writers and preachers who make much use of the older technical terms of our ancient theology often seem to be out of touch with reality: they speak a tongue that has become foreign to the people. For this misfortune, no doubt, there is an obvious remedy—to give up the use of technical terms. But no science can abjure the use of technical terms, and the science of Christian theology ought to be able to present its subject in the current coinage of the thought of the day. A radical change of terminology is as much needed to-day if Christian theology is to hold its own as a coherent system with the learned, as a further extension of the method of interpretation already in vogue in regard to some clauses of the Apostles' Creed is needed, before the unity and coherence of all its clauses can be restored. The

---

[1] It is not the plan of this book to treat of these philosophical statements, except incidentally; but I would warmly commend to the attention of those who do not know it Dr. A. C. M'Giffert's book *The Rise of Modern Religious Ideas* (New York, The Macmillan Company, 1915), and Dr. W. Adams Brown's *Christian Theology in Outline* (Edinburgh, T. & T. Clark, 1907), and *Modern Theology and the Preaching of the Gospel* (New York, Charles Scribner's Sons, 1914).

process of re-interpretation has already gone too far for any lesser remedy. It has undoubtedly destroyed for ever the unity of the Creed as a work of art, if the central and dominant clause, and the clause "he rose again from the dead", are to be held to be incapable of similar re-interpretation. It would be as if we took a picture of some old-world hero, painted from the life, and left our central figure in the costume of the period, but painted in afresh the attendants and the background and all the properties to be characteristic of the fashion and manner of life of the twentieth century. So it is with the Creed. We are left with something incoherent, incongruous, all out of focus and perspective, if we cannot apply to the whole the principle of interpretation which we allow ourselves to apply to parts.

When we do apply this principle, the unity of the faith that the Creed expresses, and the underlying harmony of clause after clause, are seen to be so real that comment on the various clauses and sections cannot be made without a good deal of repetition.

III

[I BELIEVE] "IN JESUS CHRIST HIS ONLY SON OUR LORD"

THERE is nothing specifically 'Christian' in believing in GOD. The faith of a 'Christian' in GOD is determined entirely by his faith in Jesus. Any intelligent being, including the meanest or the most malign of spiritual intelligences that exist, may believe in GOD. And their GOD may be like themselves. But the GOD in whom 'Christians' believe is the GOD on communion with whom the whole life and being of Jesus depended. It is, in a word, His GOD: the GOD of a man who played the part which we know He played in the actual history of the world as we know it. And more than this, He is a GOD who is like Jesus Himself, a GOD of whose character the character of Jesus is the revelation. It may be an overstatement of the facts to say that the Christian knows nothing of GOD apart from Jesus, or except as seen and known in Him ; but it is with Jesus that his Christian faith in GOD begins. Jesus is its true creator.

Whether the truth of the Christian faith depends on its correspondence with the actual facts of the life of Jesus, or not, Christian Doctrine, as far back as we can trace it, has been inseparably connected with a historical person. It has always been based on the belief that Jesus really lived, was the kind of person described in the Gospels, and was crucified and rose again from the dead. It is just this belief that differentiates Christian theology, and Christian ethics too, from any other theology, or any other system of ethics.

Theology is only the account or theory that is given of GOD, and every one who believes in GOD at all has a theology, however inarticulate it may be. But of Christian theology the centre is not GOD but Jesus. The significance of the Person of Jesus is its supreme concern. He is the one fact on which Christian theology is built. All Christian doctrines, like all Christian institutions, are attempts to express and to maintain the view of human life which is embodied in Him; and any statement of Christian Doctrine must begin with Him—who and what He was: the historical Person Jesus who once in the history of the world lived among men as man.[1]

---

[1] We are concerned with the contents rather than the truth of the faith of a Christian, and therefore we need not enter on the question recently raised as to whether the working value of belief in 'the Christ of faith' does not sufficiently attest and guarantee the truth of the belief, altogether apart from the actual facts about 'the Jesus of

So the real centre of the Apostles' Creed is to be found in the clauses which express belief about Him. The Christian conception of GOD is formed by a process of reasoning back from belief about Jesus, and all the later clauses of the Creed derive their meaning from the belief about Him which is expressed in the central part of the Creed. The doctrine of the Church and the Sacraments does not depend on their having been founded or instituted by Jesus, but rather on the doctrine of the Incarnation, which itself could never have arisen without belief in the Resurrection. And on belief in the resurrection of Jesus Himself depends the belief of the Church

---

history'—so that Christian Doctrine might be true whatever its origin was, even though it had no basis in things that actually happened. From this point of view the doctrine of the Incarnation might be true, even if Jesus never lived at all ; if there never was a real person, not as the Gospels pourtray our Lord, of course, but a real person to become by a wonderful process of transfiguration the Jesus of the Gospels. With regard to this question there are only two remarks to be made that are germane to our subject. The reality of the existence of Jesus is central in the faith of a Christian, just because He is conceived as the personal incarnation of the personality of GOD. If He did not really exist, there has not been made that manifestation of GOD to men, on belief in which the whole Christian doctrine of GOD depends. And again, it must be remarked that it is not from those who have entered most fully into the critical study of the Gospels that doubts about the existence of Jesus come. Such students may think that the historical Jesus has been transfigured by later belief into something far less human and natural than He really was ; but the more human and natural He becomes in the crucible of critical study, the clearer also the proofs of His real existence become. 'Criticism' of Christian 'origins' gives a fatal blow to the theory that Jesus never lived. It can only stand up at all to the traditional conception of the facts ; and even then it cannot hold its ground.

in the resurrection of the dead and the life of the world to come.

All the latter articles of the Creed are thus mere consequences of the articles on the Person and experiences of Jesus. The prefatory statement of belief in GOD the Father is for Christian theology logically misplaced — it is at least proleptic: it anticipates the following clauses and gets its meaning from them. Perhaps it owes its place in the forefront of the Creed to the fact that belief in one GOD was shared by Jews and in some degree by many of the philosophers of other races. So, though the Christian conception of the 'one GOD' soon came to be *sui generis*, there was this much common ground between Christians and others.[1] Yet the difference between the Christian and other conceptions of GOD is at least as deep as any likeness that there is between them. Christian experience was from a very early time in more or less conscious opposition to the current Jewish and philosophical conceptions of the unity of GOD; and the record of the doctrinal controversies of the earliest centuries is the record of the stages by which this Christian consciousness assumed a definite form and made itself good against unitarian conceptions that would

---

[1] St. Paul's address at Athens is an instance of the use that might be made of this common ground. Later Christian 'apologies' generally make it the basis of their argument, sometimes in rather startling ways.

have found a place for Christ as Revealer, Redeemer, Lord, outside the Being of GOD. The Church as a whole had no disposition to discourage attempts to work out answers to the pressing problems that confronted it in relation to its main convictions about Jesus. It had to compete with other old established religions and philosophies, as well as some new ones, and to justify its Creed as reasonable and coherent. It was only when solutions of problems were offered which ignored some of the *data*, whether of early tradition or of present actual experience of Christians, that those solutions were ruled out, whether better ones could be found or not. No theory was to be accepted that formally made the Lord less divine than GOD, or formally impaired the reality of His manhood. Nor was any theory adjudged heretical till it had been examined in its relation to the conviction of Christians that in Jesus there had been effected the possibility for men of real union with the supreme GOD. Christian faith insisted on seeing in the experience of Jesus in some sense the experience of GOD Himself, and could tolerate no theory of His personality that made contact with Him less than contact with GOD.

The Christian Creed, accordingly, has Christ as its centre. It does not begin with GOD. It presupposes GOD, as it presupposes self and the world. But its conception of GOD and all else in it grows out of and depends on its valuation of the Person of Jesus. Its affirmations with regard to Him are, as it were, its heart, from which the life-blood runs through all its arteries and veins, in constant movement round and round, always coming back to Him.

The first affirmation we make of Jesus is that He is the Christ. What does that mean for us to-day? It is a title of office, inseparably connected with the history and religious expectations of the Jews. So far as we can discern the consciousness of Jesus in His life on earth it would appear that the sense of sonship was the original and the constant and continuous element in His experience, the background of His thought and the directing force of His will, as well as the ground of His serenity and strength. But the sense of mission went with it, and grew more specialized, till the conviction came to Him that the part assigned Him was that of the vague and mysterious figure to whose coming the sacred Scriptures and Apocalypses of His people pointed. The belief that the rôle of Messiah was to be His seems to have been a secret shared only with His most intimate disciples. His open allusions to it were always couched in ambiguous language by the aid of the title 'the Son of Man', of whom He spoke in the third person, leaving identification free. That He believed Himself to be Messiah was probably the secret that Judas sold. At His Trial even a hostile court could get no evidence on which to prove the charge. The evidence of His 'blasphemy' was furnished at last by His own assent.[1] The Crucifixion shattered the belief for the few who shared it. The Resurrection revived it, and scrutiny of the Scriptures removed the chief obstacle in the way of its wide acceptance by shewing how it behoved the Messiah to suffer. In using the title of Him in our Creed we affirm our belief in this official aspect of His personality and work. We do not inevitably share all the beliefs about the Messiah which were current at the time and are reflected in the Gospels and Epistles and Apocalypses of our own Christian Scriptures. But our use of the title means much as regards our outlook on life.

It means that we recognize a purpose of GOD running through the history of the world, dimly discerned by a few of the most reflective and creative minds of almost all peoples, but more consciously and fully apprehended by the prophets of

[1] In the synoptic Gospels, not written till the belief was universal in the Church, very few except the 'devils' are credited with insight to recognize Him as Messiah. The Fourth Gospel, as I conceive, in this respect as in some others gives us artistic theology rather than history. It represents the personality and consciousness of 'the Christ, the Son of GOD' as it was in the experience of the evangelist and the Church of his time rather than as it was realized in the years which He spent on earth as man. Historical perspective must be sacrificed when the total valuation of a great personality is the author's theme.

the people of Israel. We recognize something 'providential' in the special experience through which that people passed. We do not, like the famous heretic Marcion, maintain that the revelation of GOD'S purpose in Jesus was so entirely new and distinct as not to be truly continuous with the history of His dealings with men from the beginning of the world. We affirm the belief that human life, for the individual as for races and for the whole of mankind, is, as it were, a great school in which each and all are set to learn what is the true law of their being, and disciplined with the one and only aim of enabling them to fulfil the purpose for which they exist.

We affirm our belief that GOD'S purpose for men can be discerned by men and by whole peoples:—there is such a thing as the mind or the soul of a people. And some men and some peoples have deeper insight than others into His purpose, and are brought into closer communion with Him, and become for others the channel through which their own consciousness is quickened and their wills receive a new direction. We affirm our belief that it is part of GOD'S plan to work out His purpose for the whole world by means of such men and such peoples: the special endowments or characteristics of men and races are not entirely fortuitous or contingent; they are appointed means to a definite end. He has 'chosen' some out of the rest to act as leaders and guides to the rest: some as regards some of the ends of life, and others as regards other of those ends. He actually expresses Himself through them. If, in line with this belief, we accept as true the familiar saying that the Jews 'prepared "salvation" for the world', we do not the less believe that the Greeks and the Romans 'prepared "the world" for salvation'. It is not in any sense that would exclude other races from a share in the fulfilment of GOD'S purposes that we declare our belief that Jesus is the Christ. But we do affirm our conviction that into some of the chief characteristics of GOD and the chief constituents of the true purpose of man's life the Jews, as a race, led by their statesmen prophets, had special insight. And we affirm that in Jesus, 'after the flesh' a true descendant of those prophets, nurtured on their writings, that insight rose to its highest power. We declare that in Him GOD'S plan of guiding men through men to the fulfilment of His purpose, unhastingly, unrestingly, was accomplished as it had not been till then. He was the true exponent of the real meaning of life, its worth and its values: the true liberator of men's minds, setting them free from the false conceptions by which they had been fettered, and opening the way to achievements which before had been impossible. He was the mirror in which they might see themselves as GOD sees them, and GOD'S purpose as it is.

We affirm, too, something more than this. Christian faith is inherently and incurably optimistic. It can never despair of man and of human society, for whom and for which the Christ died—and rose again. When we state our belief in Jesus as the Christ, 'defeated' as He was in His life-time on earth, we affirm our conviction that GOD'S purpose as conceived by Him will be fulfilled. The special function of the Messiah was to inaugurate on earth the Kingdom of GOD. No conviction was more dominant, more absorbing and directive, among the early Christians than the conviction that Jesus would return to this world as the Christ in all His glory to establish this Kingdom. All He had done on earth was to manifest the inner character of the Kingdom and the qualifications required in its members, and to set in operation some of its powers for good, in anticipation of the full reality. He would surely come back to complete the work He had begun. In this expectation the first generations of His followers undoubtedly lived, and the expectation remained active in the Church till it became too closely associated with the particular form of it known as Millennialism—the belief in the Thousand Years'

Reign of Christ on earth. To this particular form of the belief many objections could be raised, and scholars late in the third century dealt it its death-blow. The belief itself, at all events as an official belief of the Church, scarcely survived the death of its definition. And a little later Augustine's influence put in its place the idea that the thousand years' reign of Christ on earth had begun already—the Kingdom was His Church of which He was the King.

No doubt the conception of the Kingdom and its coming, which early generations of Christians cherished, was catastrophic and embroidered with ideas that had no permanent worth. Some of the pictures they drew of it seem to us fanciful and wanting in spiritual tone — though the lack of intelligence may be less theirs than ours, when we interpret the sensuous imagery of their descriptions as though they were written in our own pedestrian prose. No doubt, too, as time went on and the coming of the Kingdom seemed no nearer, Christians could solace themselves with the conviction that already in the present fellowship and in the sacramental system of the Church—in the spiritualization of the earthly life which the consciousness of union with Christ in part at least effected—they were provided with some of its practical advantages and some of the superhuman possibilities it promised.

But the identification of the Church with the Kingdom, which Augustine made formally current, was a very poor substitute for the early belief. And it, in turn, could not maintain itself in the teeth of the facts of experience. The thousand years passed, and the world went on. Nothing like the new order came. So a complete *bouleversement* of the primitive Christian faith ensued. The Church settled down to the view that the Kingdom of GOD was not only, as our Lord had described its character, 'not of this world', but even in reality and substance not 'for' this world. It was, and it was to be, not 'here on homely earth', but

> yonder, worlds away,
> Where the strange and new have birth,
> That Power comes full in play.

This putting off to another life in another world of the hope of the Kingdom and the realization of its conditions is perhaps the greatest apostasy that the history of religions can disclose. As long as the primitive faith was active, the Church concerned itself to the full range of its power to remould and fashion the conventions and institutions of human society according to the ideals of the Kingdom. In the earlier days the scope of its activities was limited, and it could only deal with its own members and their relations with one another. When, in the age of Constantine, it first attained a position from which it could act more directly on the world, it still pursued this aim; but its strength was sapped by the insidious influence of the ascetic theory of life which began to pervade it; and when, by the fall of the Empire, it was left alone to create a new society, to weld the new races into a new order, to civilize and Christianize them, its efforts were controlled by a false ideal of the Kingdom and the world. To borrow the phrase of one of the first Catholic Churchmen to discover the mistake, it was not 'the Christianity of Christ' that the Church endeavoured to establish in the world. It was not true to the primitive faith expressed in the acknowledgement of Jesus as 'the Christ'.

Yet belief in the ultimate establishment of the Kingdom of GOD in the world is paramount in belief in Him as Christ. If it is the function of the faith of a Christian to affect his will and direct the activities of his life, there is no phrase in the Creed that is fraught with more immediate potency than this. The faith it denotes has been sheathed in ideas that may not be of abiding value and certainly have not held their place, though we know that 'catastrophe' plays its part in the history of men and the constitution of society as it did in the formation of the earth itself; and what the Spirit of Christ, working invisibly, accomplishes, is an achievement of His personal energy. But whatever form the faith may assume, its constant substance is the conviction that an order of life is possible in the world in which righteousness, love, and peace are sovereign. Human society can be organized on the principles of Christian ethics. What we call the laws of economics or of human nature are simply descriptions of the ways in which men have behaved in the past, when Christian ideals have not been given the chance of control. Human society has in it the immortal germs of progress towards its perfection, and the conditions of its perfectibility were described in such sayings as are collected in the Sermon on the Mount or can be gathered from the writings of the great Apostle who, more than any one else, organized Christianity for its early victories and made its future achievements possible. It will be a world-wide Society in which there is no schism and all the members have the same care one for another.

According to the religious construction of the Creed we must assign this constant and permanent value to the clause affirming faith in Jesus as Christ. We do not bring to account in connexion with this affirmation of the Creed all that 'Christ' or 'the Christ' stands for in the faith of a Christian—all the wealth of Christian experience and reflexion of which St. Paul is the classic exponent in such phrases as 'in Christ', 'that I may gain Christ', 'till Christ be formed in you', 'in Christ . . . a new creation', 'perfect in Christ', 'Christ liveth in me', 'to me life is Christ', 'the Christ our life', 'Christ in you the hope of glory', 'the unsearchable riches of Christ': for in these phrases we are taken beyond the range of creeds. Christians soon came to feel the personal name 'Jesus' inadequate for ordinary use in speaking of their Lord: it did not express what He was or their own relation to Him. Jesus living as a man in the world, the Christ of history, was 'limited' in various ways; but Jesus risen and ascended, the Christ of faith, transcends all limits; and St. Paul very seldom uses the simple name by itself. So 'the Christ' or 'Christ' ousted the noncommittal and too familiar 'Jesus' and, ceasing to be a title, became in Christian usage the personal Name. When used in this way it implies the Christian's total valuation of the Person of his Lord. To 'Christ' he can refer the whole of his religious experience: Christ is the source and the centre of his religious consciousness, the symbol of all his highest hopes for himself and the world, the personal energy that makes for the realization of the Divine in human life, the consummator of all things. But it is on a disciple's whole conviction as to the significance of the personality of Jesus that this kind of Christian mysticism depends, and, though it enters into all the most sensitive Christian experience, no express affirmation about it is made in the Creed. It is the less expansive and more definite conception which attaches to the title 'Messiah' that is predominant when we declare our belief in Jesus as Christ.

When we go on to say that Jesus is the 'only Son' of GOD, we affirm our conviction that the unique consciousness of His own relation to GOD, which is the most distinctive note or characteristic of His life, and is attested alike by His own acts and sayings and by the impression created in the minds of His intimate friends and others, was a symptom of a really existing relation. It was not 'pathological', due to an extravagant sense of the importance of His mission and the greatness of the issues: it was not merely suggested to Him by the phrases of the psalmists and prophets whose thoughts and language had been drunk in by Him and sunk deep into His mind and heart, to well up to the surface of consciousness as the expression of Himself. It was not the reflexion of an imaginary but of a real relation—a unique consciousness of a unique relation.

The relation to GOD of which He was conscious was of course conceived by Him in terms of human experience. A happy family life with its natural affections and loyalties supplied them. He felt towards GOD in the way that a loyal and loving child feels to his father while he is still a child—a child entrusted with a mission, for the carrying out of which the father, with absolute confidence in his child, can and will supply all that is needed, though the child only half understands what the mission is. This sense of sonship and mission possessed Him in a unique degree: He felt He could read the Mind and the Will of GOD as stage by stage it pleased His Father in heaven to open it out to His Son on earth, and always at every crisis of His life there came to Him the sense of strength to meet it as His Father meant and willed. He felt that He stood in a unique relation to the whole of mankind, because He had been chosen by GOD to be the vehicle to them of the revelation of His Mind and Will, to inaugurate a new era in the history of the world, and at whatever cost to Himself to be the means by which the Divine order of human society —an order of righteousness and mutual help and brotherhood—should be established.

When we affirm Him to be the 'only Son' of GOD we set the seal of our faith to the belief that what He felt about Himself He was. We know that He sought to bring all men into the fellowship of His own experience and lead them on to the same intimate sense of sonship, with its responsibility as well as its privilege. They were only blind and sinister critics who detected in His words an arrogant claim for Himself and charged Him with making GOD His Father in an exclusive sense. But we, like His early followers, feel that it is only through Him that we know the full meaning of the fatherhood of GOD and can take up our sonship, as something won for us by Him; and we need a distinctive term that sets Him by Himself. We should be wholly disloyal to Him if we doubted that the sonship to which He invited us was as full and complete as to satisfy abundantly all the desires and needs, all the potentialities, of our being. He bade us use the same address to GOD as He Himself used: not the resounding titles of Jewish and pagan worship, nor the servile or courtier-like expressions of some of our Christian prayer-books, but the simple word 'Father'.[1] If He spoke often of 'My' Father, He could also say to a man 'thy' Father, as He taught His disciples all together to say 'our' Father. He claimed no monopoly of sonship: the aim of His life was to make men worthy to be what, by the very law of their being, they were meant to be; and He would have failed entirely if He had not brought millions of men to

---

[1] The original form of the Lord's Prayer is, no doubt, more nearly represented by St. Luke's version of it, with its opening 'Father', than by St. Matthew's, with its expansive 'Our Father, which art in heaven'. The phrase that is rendered 'which art in heaven' is Matthew's own, and was probably never used by our Lord at all.

the sense of the same filial relationship to GOD that He Himself enjoyed. And yet we must mark the difference, and we do so by a phrase that says in effect that He is Son in His own right, by the prerogative of nature: a unique personality among men, even apart from any metaphysical conception of the personality of GOD. We appreciate Him as the revelation to us of that 'part' of the Divine activity which has to do with us. We learn from Him to express it as the relation of a father to his son, a loving and righteous father to a dearly loved if wayward son. In Jesus we see the perfect reflexion of this relation in a Son who was not wayward, but at every stage of His experience shewed the obedience He learnt. We believe Him to be, indeed, on earth in a human life the perfect image of the relationship in which man stands to GOD and GOD to man. And so we place Him at the very centre of the Divine activity and being, and the conception of GOD as a single Person, alone in His majesty, has to be enlarged to include, as best it may, the relations of a Father and a Son in eternal intimate communion. And at the same time and to a like extent our conception of Man and human life is at once immeasurably heightened and permanently centralized: Jesus is to us the perfect expression of the ideal of human personality which in many parts and in many ways, through all the manifold duties and interests and activities of life in the world, it is the end and business of experience to create in us. If the business of life is an art, it is also a science; and we have in Him at once the perfect model of its beauty and the exact measure of its values.

So He is also 'our Lord'. He has standardized life for us. It may be our misfortune and our fault again and again to have to confess *video meliora proboque, deteriora sequor*; but our judgement as to 'the better' can only be concerned with the application of principles to the constantly moving conditions of life with all its actions and reactions, and the incessant need of adaptation which they involve. It is 'the best' that is always before us, in so far at least as we can discover in Him or His ideals a ruling principle of thought or purpose which can be applied to the particular occasion. Those are our standards. And though we cannot achieve the ideal, yet we are faithful to our standard if we attain the nearest approximation to it that is possible in the particular complex, the particular combination of circumstances, by which we are faced at the moment, whether it be in what we call our private affairs or in matters affecting the smaller or the larger groups to which we belong. The 'better' has then the moral value of the 'best'.

OUR LORD

We must not be misled by the title 'Lord'. As it was used to Jesus in His life-time it usually meant no more than 'Sir'—a title of courtesy or of various degrees of respect. When used as an address it should constantly be so rendered in our English version of the Gospels, instead of very rarely as it is (by accident as it seems), if the true historical perspective is to be preserved.[1] But by the time when the Gospels were composed, no doubt the word as applied to Jesus had acquired a richer and deeper significance. It was a common appellation of the great ones of this world and of the unseen powers that could make or mar men's lives; and 'Lord' beyond question represents the feeling of the evangelists and the Christians for whom they wrote. Students whose business it is to trace the developement of early Christian thought and feeling have tried to mark the variations in the use of the title by Christians, and some have detected in them stages by which the influence of non-Christian associations grew, or the 'cult' of its Patron by the new religious society was established. But the elements of a 'cult' must have been present from the moment of such experiences as the Resurrection and the Ascension, and the experience of

[1] Similarly it is, of course, an anachronism to represent any one as 'worshipping' Him in His life-time, the deferential *salàm* being what occurred.

Pentecost must have confirmed them. They were inherent in 'the breaking of the bread', though St. Paul's admonitions and appeals to the Christians of Corinth shew that lower ideas connected with the common meals of non-Christian religious guilds survived in newly established groups of Christians and threatened to degrade the incipient Christian cult to their own unspiritual level. As Christian experience grew stronger and deeper, and the Christian consciousness became more sensitive and distinctive, the place in the Divine economy which it assigned to Jesus as Christ and only Son of GOD and Lord, as Revealer and Redeemer, was one that called out all the instincts of devotion; and if He was at first only the medium through whom the Christian's prayer and praise was offered to GOD, He could not but become Himself in virtue of such close association a sharer in it and an object of it. The Friend and Master of the first generation became the Divine Lord of the next; and in using of Him in the Apostles' Creed the words 'our Lord' we own that He stands in this relation to us: they are the natural expression of our devotional attitude to Him, as One exalted high above us, our representative at the very source of the love and power on which we depend and the ideals which are to us the spring and sustenance of all right thought and action, able as well as willing to put into motion on our behalf that love and energy of GOD of which He is to us not only the medium but the personalization.

The words 'our Lord' thus do imply the cult. Our thanksgiving and praise are due to Him. And the prayer that we send up to GOD, even the petitions, are as naturally addressed to Him whom we know, who personalizes GOD and makes Him real to us, as to the Father to whom He taught men to pray in the spirit of His own prayers as man. Prayer made to Him is made to the GOD He revealed. In former times men thought it of the first importance to know the name of the GOD who could do what they wanted, and to be able to send their prayer in the right form and with the exact address and titles. Christians believe they have the right address and the name, and, what is equally important, they know the form. Prayers in the form and the spirit of Jesus reach His GOD, whether they are addressed to Him by the title of Father or of Son. For prayer in any other spirit or any other form than this there is no kind of 'Christian' justification. The prayer of a Christian is always the prayer of a free personality seeking to unfold and realize its best capacities, or its highest good as it understands it, in fellowship with its own Creator conceived as knowing and willing its highest good and perfection. It is seeking for itself, or for other personalities like itself, insight into the meaning of its past or present experience to enable it to use its opportunities aright, with courage both to endure and to dare. It is its effort to range itself and others on the side of the good, the beautiful, and the true, and so add to its power to overcome the evil, the ugly, and the false in human life. It is a conscious endeavour to produce in itself and in others the particular reaction on experience which will further, instead of impeding, the working out of the purpose of GOD. It is a travesty of Christian prayer that looks to GOD to do things for us that we can do for ourselves. To 'leave it to GOD' is to renounce the birthright which belongs to us of consciously working with Him for His ends, and to ignore the first condition and the *raison d'être* of a free personality. All the resources at our own disposal must be used, and prayer must be conditioned and motived by recognition of the truth implied in the doctrine of the Incarnation, that GOD works in the world of our experience effectively only through men. "They that worship GOD must worship Him in spirit and in truth." The worship implied in the title 'our Lord' is the worship of the spiritual and the true (the good and the beautiful) made actual in human life in Him.

But there is also another religious affirmation that we make in using the words 'our Lord'. If the title implies that He represents to us GOD and the Divine ideal for men, a relationship in which He seems to be remote, it also implies a close and, as it were, domestic connexion between Him and us. The meaning which the Greek word constantly has in the New Testament is one which reflects perhaps the Divine intention in the education of the race, but certainly the economic conditions of ordinary life as men have made them. It is the 'master' with 'his' man. We declare ourselves 'the men' of Jesus Christ, owning our allegiance to Him and our duty of service. We acknowledge that it is our business not only to reverence Him and admire His ideals at a distance, but to try to realize them: to try to fashion our own lives and the common life of our group in harmony with them. It is a social responsibility that we acknowledge, as well as a personal loyalty to Him. He is 'our' Master, whose mind and will are to be the common mind and will of our society, which is to represent as nearly as possible in its organization the ideal order which He called the Kingdom of GOD.[1]

[1] In connexion with these clauses of the Creed it is a pleasure to be able to refer students to Dr. C. Anderson Scott's recently published *Dominus Noster* (Cambridge, W. Heffer and Sons, 1918), though I cannot myself endorse all that he says.

F

IV

"WHO WAS CONCEIVED BY THE HOLY GHOST, BORN OF THE VIRGIN MARY"

THE Creed goes on to expand the doctrine of the Sonship and the Lordship of Jesus Christ by a statement as to the mode in which He entered on the human life He lived.

The genuine Creed of Nicaea (A.D. 325)—the only one of our three Creeds which was compiled by a General Council of the Church—the Creed, moreover, which was intended to be used as a test of orthodoxy in bishops—did not contain this clause or any like it, rich as it was in other phrases, popular and scientific, affirming the full Godhead of the Son. Nor, apparently, had it a place in the old baptismal Creed of Caesarea, on which the new and more technical Creed of Nicaea was based. Nor, yet again, does the most scientific of all our Creeds, the 'Athanasian', contain any reference to it. So far as these facts go by themselves,[1] it would appear

[1] They are facts to which, I think, attention should be paid :—facts, too, which seem to have escaped the notice of some divines of to-day.

BORN OF THE VIRGIN MARY

that the claims of orthodoxy might still be satisfied by a profession of faith in terms which do not allude to the manner of our Lord's Nativity. But that is the full extent of the inference that can fairly be drawn from the facts. The clause, or one to the same effect, was already long established, it seems, in the baptismal Creeds of the West, and it may have been contained in similar Eastern Creeds from an early date. In any case there is no doubt of the great antiquity of the belief as to the miraculous mode of our Lord's birth. If we may take the addresses of St. Peter recorded in the Acts of the Apostles as historical and typical, we must admit

---

Personally, as a student of the developement of Christian Doctrine and its many forms of expression, I may be allowed to say that I much prefer to state my own beliefs, 'theological' and 'Christological', in the terms of the Athanasian Creed. It is the only Creed that precludes the tritheistic ideas always latent in the faith of Christians, and really states the Trinitarian—that is, the Christian—doctrine of GOD. The modern equivalents of its terms, into which one mentally translates them, are not far to seek. Though clearly the work of a single mind, that of a scholar in his study, laboriously evolved, it expresses, I am sure, the genuine theological mind of the Church, and gives the true intellectual answer to the many misleading ideas to which it refers. To the trained theologian its assertions on these points ring as true to-day as ever. But only he can really make its terms his own. They are merely *hocus-pocus* to any one else. I am sure that it expresses also the genuine mind of the official Church of the past as to the fate in store for 'heretics', which it desired to hold *in terrorem* before its members. I think there is some ground for a plea that in this respect the heart of the official Church was larger than its mind. But even the mind of the official Church of England is enlarged towards heretics to-day, and interpretation of this part of the Creed has become not only free, but even (theologically speaking) licentious.

that the belief had no place in the earliest public preaching of the Gospel. But, then, every careful reader knows that the doctrine about Jesus which those addresses indicate is very far from being the full doctrine of the Incarnation; and we cannot assign an exact date to the time at which the belief first became so generally accepted among Christians as to be able to exert any influence on their doctrine. Yet that is a question with which we must attempt to deal.

For our present purpose we have no interest in any conclusion as to the evidence for or against the historical credibility of the tradition itself. It is of course equally impossible to 'prove' it true or to 'prove' it false; and belief in it depends on other considerations than those of historical evidence, even when the term 'historical' is given its widest range.[1] The only question that concerns us for our present purpose is this: Was an estimate of the significance of Jesus which we can regard as substantially the same as the doctrine of the Incarnation arrived at

---

[1] I do not desire to obtrude my own opinions on such points as these, which do not seem to me to be central in the faith of a Christian. But it seems right that I should state my belief that the strictly historical evidence is altogether insufficient to establish the supposed fact, and that the other considerations to which I refer are only weighty enough to have an inhibitive force—to forbid denial and suggest a state of suspense of judgement. In that state of suspense I am content to remain: but the discussion that follows will shew that I can find no place for the supposed fact in connexion with the doctrine of the Incarnation, and cannot say that I believe it.

independently of the belief in His miraculous conception? or was this belief either the underlying basis of every such estimate when it was formed, or at all events—so far as we have means of judging—so indissolubly connected with it, that we are justified in saying that as far as our evidence goes the high doctrine (not indicated in Acts at a time when the belief could not have been 'current') was never held apart from the belief as to the manner of the Birth?

I desire to emphasize the question in this form, with the single purpose of discovering whether there were in early times, as there certainly are to-day, any teachers who held the highest doctrine of our Lord's Person while ignoring the story of His Nativity, whether known to them or not. If so, there would be confirmation for the suggestion that it is belief in the doctrine of the Incarnation, as expressed for example in the original Creed of Nicaea, rather than belief in the miraculous conception, as stated in the Apostles' Creed, that should be regarded as the token of the faith of a Christian.

Unfortunately the question I have framed is not one to which a certain answer can be given. But the evidence of the New Testament that the doctrine grew up independently of the belief is, I think, far stronger than it is usually admitted to be. I do not rely on the mere fact that the belief is only stated in the prologue to the Gospels of St. Luke and St.

Matthew.[1] Nor, again, should I attach much weight to the fact that we had a good deal of early Christian literature that did not allude to it, especially if it was of an 'occasional' character dealing especially with practical questions, and presupposing a background of oral teaching; and this is the case with many of the writings that make up the New Testament, and with the Letter of St. Clement that had a place in some early Christian Bibles. It would not be a decisive fact that any one might read through a collection of such writings and get no inkling that such a belief was current. The

[1] How widely the belief was current, if really 'current' at all, when St. Luke wrote his Gospel, there is no evidence to shew; nor, again, how quickly and how widely the belief, when current, spread. A good summary of modern criticism of the narratives of the Nativity in the Gospels will be found in J. Moffatt, *An Introduction to the Literature of the New Testament* (T. & T. Clark, 1911), or, more readably, in Hastings' *Dictionary of Christ and the Gospels*, articles 'The Birth of Christ' and 'Virgin Birth'. Here also will be found some discussion of the theory that 'the only reference to the Virgin Birth in the Third Gospel' is in chap. ii. verses 34, 35, and that these verses are a later interpolation. Any one who wishes to examine the narratives in detail can do so with the guidance of these books, in which references to the extensive literature of the subject are given. I would only add that in my own judgement the theory of interpolation, which admittedly lacks all positive evidence, breaks down on examination, and we must assume that St. Luke himself narrated a miraculous conception and birth of our Lord, as St. Matthew's Gospel certainly does. St. Luke is a master of the art of poetic handling of a theme. One can hardly conceive of his Gospel shorn of this its entirely congruous beginning. He was certainly no spiritualist or mystic, though he is the only evangelist who betrays an interest in the psychology of his subject. For him, a medical man as well as an artist, a unique personality needed a unique origination. On this question see *infra*, pp. 90 *ff*.

BORN OF THE VIRGIN MARY

argument from silence is far too precarious to be depended on in such a case. It only becomes of real weight when we can say that a writer must have alluded to a particular fact if he had known it, or to a belief if it had been his own; and we are very seldom able to use the word 'must'.

Yet, if the belief under consideration is of the importance which some would attribute to it to-day, it is a remarkable fact that it is not mentioned in connexion with any of the deepest teaching contained in the New Testament. In the Letters of St. Paul, the Epistle to the Hebrews, and the Gospel and Epistles of St. John, we have three sets of writings in which distinct and carefully reasoned appreciations of the significance of the same Person are set before us. They clearly come from men of very different minds and temperaments and antecedents, all of them learned and profound thinkers, and all of them concerned to commend by argument and various kinds of demonstration the highest doctrine about our Lord that the New Testament contains. Yet nowhere is there even a suggestion of any argument or proof to be derived from the mode of His birth. Like all close students of thoughts and words I hesitate to say that nowhere can the remotest reference to it be found, but I must express my conviction that it is not alluded to in the very few passages in which microscopic examination has been able to detect it (these passages are discussed in a note at the end of this chapter).

The writer to the Hebrews might, indeed, have deliberately avoided it, because the main stress of his argument falls on the genuinely human experience by which Jesus became qualified to be the High Priest of humanity, and won the glory of being the representative of the race of men in the presence of GOD, having passed to the Holy of Holies through the tabernacle which His living manhood furnished for Him. The Epistle to the Hebrews, in spite of the antiquarian form of its thought and phraseology, is perhaps in substance the most human and the most 'modern' of all the books of the New Testament. The writer is the first of whom we know to face the problem of a suffering Redeemer as one for which a deeper answer must be found than had, till then, been given. And he certainly would not have been helped to his solution, or in his argument, by any reference to a belief that the Person whom he describes as 'taken from men' and 'appointed on behalf of men', in order that He might have full sympathy with them, had an unparalleled beginning of His human life. If he knew of the belief, he put it entirely aside as useless to him for his purpose. It had no bearing on the doctrine which he desired to establish—the doctrine which makes the most intimate appeal to the minds as well as the hearts of many Christian Churchmen, and gives an early answer to the question often asked in later times, *Cur Deus homo?* that is likely to approve itself as of abiding worth when other answers are forgotten.

St. Paul, on the other hand, was one whose mind was so fixed on the Christ of his own experience that he cared comparatively little about the details of His life on earth apart from His actual Passion and Resurrection — those details which were all-important to the writer to the Hebrews. It was not Jesus 'after the flesh', but Jesus ascended, who was first revealed to him in living strength and activity. He was clear that the Person who was the centre and mainspring of his own new consciousness and life had, of His own free-will, laid aside the Divine state of existence which was His, and condescended to be born of a woman and come as man into the world. He is emphatic, sometimes amazingly emphatic, as to the completeness of the change of state. But he shews no kind of interest in any question concerning the way in which it was effected. There is no sign that his lofty doctrine, or any part of his argument, in any way depended on the belief that in becoming man the Son of GOD had no human father, or that he would have regarded such a belief as a corollary to his doctrine. The mystery of GOD in Christ reconciling the world to

Himself did not demand it, and the Pauline doctrine, to the full extent to which his letters give abundant witness, may be accepted to-day on the grounds on which he himself appears to have based it.

It is, however, when we come to the Johannine writings that the absence of all reference to the belief is most remarkable. For by the time the Fourth Gospel was written it is almost certain that the belief was current at all events in some Christian circles. There is good reason to suppose that the author knew the Gospels of St. Mark and St. Luke. It is a well-based theory, widely held by students of his Gospel, that he frequently 'intervenes' to correct or to supplement the narratives of his predecessors in the difficult task of presenting the full truth about Jesus. Deliberately and expressly he sets himself to convince his readers 'that Jesus is the Christ, the Son of GOD' (xx. 31), and he identifies Him with the Logos who was in the beginning and was with GOD and was GOD (i. 1), who, he proclaims, 'became flesh' and was manifested in Jesus: Jesus was the Logos incarnate. While the other evangelists appear to adopt a simple and straightforward method of historical narration of the chief incidents and sayings which were known to them, and let them speak for themselves as it were, the author of the Fourth Gospel presents us with a selection of incidents carefully chosen and expressly designed to illustrate the real personality of his subject Jesus. Each of them is a 'sign', or symbol, or evidence, of what He really is. The author calls special attention to their symbolical significance, and in most cases uses them as the 'text' of long discourses in which the various attributes and characteristics of the Person represented as speaking are expounded. The selection even of small details for narration is made with a view to their value as illustrative of some point in the discourse or some trait in the personality which is to be noted.

They are all, it is true, what we call 'miracles', done by Jesus, to manifest His 'glory'. They are pressed upon the reader as signs of what He is in Himself. Through them His true nature and being is indicated. His Mother plays a part in the narrative of the first of these signs and in the narrative of the closing hours of His life on earth. Women are conspicuous in other scenes in the Gospel as vehicles through which the revelation of Himself is made. The reality of His manhood, His dependence on His Father in heaven, is emphasized, and at the same time His real oneness with the Father. Yet the 'sign' of what He was which is believed to be furnished by the manner of His birth is left unnoticed. His birth was not, of course, strictly speaking, something which 'Jesus' did; but it was clearly, according to the doctrine of St. John, an act of the Logos, with whom Jesus is identified: "The Logos became flesh."

We should go farther than the nature of the evidence allows us to go, if we drew the inference that the author of the Gospel deliberately intended tacitly to discredit the belief which was probably already current. But, if the evidence of his Gospel is allowed any weight at all, when the special purpose and the plan of it is considered, we can hardly escape the conclusion that he did not find in what he knew about the manner of our Lord's birth any evidence of what He was which he could offer to convince men that the doctrine of the Incarnation was the true explanation of the facts. The doctrine of the Incarnation, as expounded in the Fourth Gospel, does not need the support of St. Luke's account of the Nativity. It stands on a different level, and it stands by its own strength.

We are therefore, after all, able to give an answer which, if not certain, is at least highly probable, to the question which I ventured to say is the only one that really concerns us for our present purpose. An estimate of the significance of Jesus, as regards His personality and His relation to GOD and to men, substantially the same as that which is expressed by the doctrine of the Incarnation, is in our hands from the pens of three distinct writers, each with a special genius of his own—the most creative and the most normative of all the early interpreters of Jesus in terms of the highest religious thought of the different 'schools' of thought of the time. So far as the evidence goes, none of them connected his interpretation of Him, or the argument by which he sought to press it home, with the belief that He had no human father.

We are accustomed to speak of the congruity of that belief with the high doctrine which we maintain about our Lord. It is notorious, however, that the belief led in the past, and easily leads to-day, to denial of the reality of His manhood. And yet, on the other hand, students of the history of Doctrine know that there were thinkers in the past who fell far short of belief in our Lord's Godhead and rejected the belief in His pre-existence, and nevertheless accepted His miraculous birth as a fact:—so far were they from the point of view of Christians of later times who regard the miraculous birth as the chief evidence of the doctrine of the Incarnation and propound the dilemma '*Either* a miraculous birth *or* no Incarnation'. To these early thinkers the miraculous birth, which they readily accepted as part of the tradition, did not even suggest an Incarnation or the Christian conception of GOD. In later times, too, the belief was one of the strongest supports of the ascetic theory of life, which as a theory, whatever it might be in practice, can hardly be reconciled with the doctrine of the Incarnation.

There is an entire absence of evidence that the belief would have been felt to be congruous with the lines of thought pursued by the three great Christian philosophers of the New Testament. The first of the second-century theologians—the noble martyr Ignatius—seems to regard the manner of birth as a kind of *camouflage* designed to deceive the Devil; and he was followed in this estimate of its purpose by subtler theologians than himself.

It is notorious also that the belief lacks congruity with much of the best religious philosophy of our own time. It is questionable whether any Christian philosopher to-day would regard it as congruous with his Christian faith as a whole if it had not been instilled into him before he knew what it meant. The belief itself first appears in a poetic setting in the most artistic of our Gospels. Its place is in the poetry of our religion, and it is a shame to turn it into prose. In its proper place it expresses the same valuation of the facts which on another plane of emotion and thought the doctrine of the Incarnation expresses. It is this doctrine for which it stands in the Apostles' Creed.

Again let me say that I am not treating of the credibility of the tradition but only discussing the question of the relation between the belief and the doctrine of the Incarnation. I have given reasons for my belief that there was at first no inherent connexion between the two. I am confident that for Christians who reason out their faith there is no inherent connexion to-day.

They do not base their faith in Jesus as the Christ, as Lord, as Son of GOD and Redeemer of men; as being the full manifestation of the character and being of GOD under the conditions of our human life in the world, and at the same time the revelation to men of the ideal of that human life in the world, in the light of which alone men and women singly and human society as a whole can steadily move towards the fulfilment of GOD'S purpose:—they do not base this their unique faith in Him on the supposed fact of His having come into the world in a way which was unparalleled. Rather they reach this faith through the evidence of His personality and life as a whole:—His firm conviction of the Fatherhood of GOD and His loving purpose for mankind, His consciousness of instant dependence on Him and intimate communion with Him, the spiritual insight of His teaching, His power over men's souls and wills, drawing them to Him and through Him to a consciousness of GOD like His; a power which grew greater after His death than it had been in His life-time, the power which shewed itself in the Resurrection and has been experienced by millions since; the spiritual miracles which He has wrought, miracles which have happened and are happening day by day among those who have come to believe in Him. This is the real bed-rock of faith in Him: the Jesus of history in the larger sense of history; the *gesta Christi*, all that the belief has accomplished; Christian experience, individual and collective, from the beginning until now.

It is on this kind of evidence that belief in the Incarnation is based, and the record of it is the real 'history' of Jesus, constant and continuous. He has shewn Himself to be an abiding power in the world, an active spiritual force comparable with no other. On evidence of this kind we realize His uniqueness among men; we know the conviction He had that He was able to reveal GOD to men as none other had been able; we know the claims He made on men's loyalty and allegiance to Himself, and we know the power He has shewn to vindicate and justify those claims; and so we come to a real, a living faith in His Lordship and Godhead. We never need to raise the question, 'How can these things be?' When it is raised, the true answer is, 'Come and see', or 'Follow thou me'. It is no more now than it was at the beginning of the Gospel, 'He was born of a virgin.'

But the question arises, Surely a belief of such a character would never have been retained so long unless it corresponded with at least some vital element of the doctrine of the Incarnation. I think that there are other reasons for the retention of a belief so realistic, so decorative, so intertwined from an early date with the emotional expression of the faith of the Church and its practice. Yet I believe there are many Christians to-day who do associate their faith in the moral perfection of our Lord's human life with their belief that He had no human father, and the grounds for such an association must be sympathetically considered.

First we are bound to note that the belief in our Lord's moral perfection as Man often implies and goes with the belief that His human nature was not the same as ours. But the Catholic doctrine is that our Lord was 'perfect man', in the sense that His manhood was whole and complete, lacking in nothing that is essential to manhood. The phrase of the Athanasian Creed does not mean what we mean by 'morally' perfect. It negatives the idea that any of the normal constituents of manhood were wanting in Him. And, indeed, this part of the Catholic doctrine of the Incarnation has been held to be inconsistent with the belief that our Lord had no human father. It has been urged in recent years by at least two English clergymen that a 'supernatural' birth would destroy the reality of the manhood, and thus that the Church has maintained two contradictory beliefs, the one exclusive of the other: unless our Lord had a human father, He could not really have been 'perfect man'.

I do not think that this argument has much weight. It seems to reflect too narrowly 'masculine' a mind. Woman, as much as man, possesses all the properties of human nature; and if she could conceive a child by some other than the ordinary process, there can be no doubt that she would transmit those properties of human nature to her offspring. He who is born of woman is man. No woman, no mother, could doubt it; nor could she regard that which was born into the world of her as other than her child, part of her own substance or being or nature. He would be fully human.[1] We must, I am sure, reject this negative argument as to the relation between the belief and the doctrine.

But can we allow more weight to another, positive, argument as to the religious value of the belief which has long been current in Christian thought? The birth from a Virgin was necessary, it has been held, in order that 'the entail of sin' might be cut off, and the Saviour of men be Himself 'without sin'.

For a statement of this theory we may refer to the words of Pearson, one of the most famous

---

[1] And surely there would be no kind of slur cast by the belief on human birth and generation. Though, according to it, the natural order was for once transcended, yet the belief, that the Son of GOD in becoming man had a human parent, hallows parentage.

occupants of the Lady Margaret's Chair, renowned for his learning in the Caroline age of learned divines, and still known by his elaborate work on the Creed, which most candidates for ordination in the Church of England are still, very rightly, set to study. The theory is summed up in the sentence, " Our High Priest is 'separate from sinners' not only in the actions of his life, but *in the production of his nature*." [1]

Now, it has been ill-naturedly said of Pearson that he was a much better divine than bishop. I do not know whether that was true, judged by the standards of the time. A man may, perhaps, be a good bishop although an indifferent divine. But I am afraid we must confess that, judged by the knowledge of to-day, Pearson was a very bad biologist.

" Whereas *we* draw something of corruption and contamination . . . from the first Adam; our Saviour received the same nature without any culpable inclination, because born of a Virgin. . . ." That statement depends on a very ancient idea that the father only is the parent of the child (an idea, it may be said in passing, which still survives hidden behind some of our laws which ignore the mother's rights in her own children). But we know now that this idea is not in accordance with the facts. The

[1] *An Exposition of the Creed*, art. iii. chap. iii. § 176.

mother contributes to the being, the personality, of the child as much as does the father. And *she* is as much a child of the first Adam as is the father. She draws as much of " corruption and contamination . . . from the first Adam" as does he; and the taint of original sin could as well be transmitted by one parent as by two.

If, therefore, the entail of sin was cut off at all, it was not by the process of "the production of [our Lord's human] nature", or "without seminal traduction" from His Mother. So that, unless we are to pile miracle upon miracle, we must give up the argument that the miraculous mode of His conception guarantees the sinlessness of our Lord as man.

When I say 'pile miracle upon miracle', I refer to an old theory of the undivided Church, generally accepted (though not unchallenged) from at least the beginning of the third century, and to a modern theory formally promulgated by the Church of Rome for the first time some sixty years ago. The old theory is this: It was not enough for the devotional instincts of the Church that there should be no human father, that the conception should be supernatural; the actual birth itself was declared to be supernatural, non-human, without loss of the virginity of the Mother; and the perpetual virginity of the Mother of the Lord became a fixed belief. But even that was not enough, and we come naturally to the modern theory. As His human nature was derived from His Mother's human nature, that Mother's human nature must itself have been free from sin, and so she too must have been miraculously conceived; and the doctrine of the immaculate conception of the Virgin Mary herself carries back the wonder to the beginning of her own life too. There is no flaw in the logic.

We shall do well, therefore, to abandon the theory that the sinlessness of our Lord depends on the doctrine "conceived by the Holy Ghost", or is in any way secured by the belief that He had, as man, no father. According to Catholic doctrine He had a human soul and a human will, which belonged to the human nature and body derived from His Mother; and these were all subject to the hopes and the fears, the joys and the sorrows, the temptations and the sufferings which human beings experience. In His human life He passed through the course of growth and developement of human faculties which is incidental to a genuine human experience. The Gospels declare this plainly, and it is the special aim of the Epistle to the Hebrews to shew that it was just this human experience that enabled Him to become the Saviour and High Priest of men— their leader and guide, because He felt the full force of their temptations, and passed through them unpolluted by them. He who falls into sin gives way and yields before he has felt the full force of the temptation.

The doctrine that our Lord was able to do this because His human nature was, in its very origin, sinless, incapable of feeling sinful inclination, seems to be untrue to the history of the Gospels and to invalidate the whole argument of the Epistle to the Hebrews. And, perhaps worse than this, it makes our Lord in no true sense an Example and Leader for other men in their course through life—a point which has often been seized by men, who excuse themselves from moral effort on the plea that our Lord, who is set before them as an ideal, was sinless by His very nature.

But it may be said that the special idea of an 'entail of sin' is not a living idea to-day. Yet such ideas die hard. The doctrine of 'original sin', on which it depends, is firmly embedded in common Christian teaching, and has not yet been restated to the people, though enough of expert knowledge has filtered through to them to shake their confidence in it. And as regards the Person of our Lord and His manhood there survive, I believe, far and wide, ideas derived from the ancient doctrine of sin in a form in which few thinking men now believe it and few theologians would state it. So it is not 'slaying the slain' to consider the question whether belief in our Lord's birth from a Virgin guarantees belief in His freedom from sin throughout His life as Man.

We are led, I think, to the conclusion that it can only do so for those whose 'metaphysic' and 'psychology' of life is either different from that which prevails to-day, or else not consciously brought into relation with their religious traditions and beliefs. The conception has value when we think of reality and life in terms of substance and fixed quantities, each with its special permanent qualities, when qualities themselves become identified with quantities. It ceases to be an expression of our actual consciousness when life is realized by us rather as something purposive and mobile, under the form of its manifestations, and we think in terms of energy and will and character. With the older static conception which held the ground for centuries the connexion between the two beliefs is easily apparent. It is not so according to the dynamic conceptions of personality and life and ethical attainment by which our thought is inevitably fashioned to-day, with which, accordingly, our religious beliefs, to be real, must correspond. 'Goodness', 'sinlessness', we know is not something which can be acquired once for all and retained as a possession for ever, in this life at all events. And the ethical appeal of the Gospel is immeasurably more cogent when its central Figure is seen as a Person whose goodness or sinlessness in His human life on earth was subject to the dynamic of all that life's experiences, and was not guaranteed by His possession of a 'human nature' which was not really like ours, as it would not be if 'impeccability' could be predicated of it.[1]

The belief that He Himself in His life in the world was sinless; that His human will was always directed to the fulfilment of His Father's will, into which He had unerring though not always instantaneous insight—His attitude often that of expectancy and waiting on events; that He did nothing 'without the Father'; that He never swerved from the path by which the perfection of the Father's purpose for Him was to be attained: all this, no doubt, is at least implied in the doctrine of the Incarnation. But the belief that it is true of Him is derived not from any theory as to the manner of His birth, but from the evidence of His life.

We must reject, therefore, the argument that belief in the literal sense of the clause in the Creed as to His birth has any particular connexion with

---

[1] For ancient discussions of the question whether our Lord's human nature was human nature as originally created, or that nature as it was after the Fall of man, I must be allowed to refer to a Note in my *Early History of Christian Doctrine*, pp. 250-252, and a Note by Dr. Srawley in *The Journal of Theological Studies*, vol. vii. pp. 434-441. The whole discussion, of course, depends on the conception of 'human nature' as a substance originally created 'without sin' and capable of being transmuted as a whole, and it is now of interest only to professional theologians and antiquarians.

BORN OF THE VIRGIN MARY

belief in His ethical perfection or goodness or sinlessness; and we can proceed to consider whether the belief in any way confirms the doctrine or follows on it as a natural if not inevitable inference from it.

In considering this question, abjuring for the moment all statements of the doctrine that employ terminology that is not scriptural, let us turn rather to the Fourth Gospel and St. Paul.

We have already noted that not a single phrase can be found in either the Johannine or the Pauline writings that inevitably postulates the supernatural birth of our Lord, and that we cannot rule out the possibility that neither writer shared the belief. But in any case He was to them a 'supernatural' Person. To the author of the Fourth Gospel He was a Person who had Divine existence as the Logos, or the only-begotten GOD, from the beginning, before He entered on His human life. This theory of Divine pre-existence was shared independently by St. Paul, expressly stated by him on occasion—not as a new doctrine, but as something so generally believed that he could refer to it casually when he wanted an illustration to enforce his teaching on the subject of Christian humility and brotherly service [1] —and implied again and again. It certainly under-

---

[1] Phil. ii. 1 ff.; and again, 2 Cor. viii. 9—the riches of which He stripped Himself in order by His poverty to enrich the world.

lies his analogy between the first man, who was from the earth earthy, and the second man, who was from heaven (1 Cor. xv. 47). His whole conception seems to be determined by the thought that in and with Jesus something entirely new came into the world, a new vital energy, a new force or power of GOD, which was GOD'S free gift to men—itself a new creation which resulted in the new creation of all who by faith were made one with Him who was the representative of a new race of men, the firstborn among many brethren. There was 'a new start' in the moral order, a new consciousness and potency. This introduction of a new element into human experience seems to be of the essence of the Pauline as of the Johannine doctrine of Incarnation. It does not necessarily foreclose a perfectly natural human developement of the Child born into the conditions of human life, to go through a natural course of self-realization, with a gradually growing consciousness not only of His mission but of Himself. It requires the continuity of His manhood with the manhood which was to be re-created. That continuity is secured by His generation in and of a human Mother. But it also implies something discontinuous.

It may be true that every child that is born into the world is in a true sense a new creation; the conditions requisite for the origination of life are unknown to us; it remains an unsolved enigma. If it is true, as we believe, that the Holy Spirit of GOD is the Giver of Life, it must be true that every child is "conceived by the Holy Ghost". Every new creation must be His work. Yet in case of human birth each such new creation is but one in an unbroken series, extending far back to innumerable progenitors: and a real break in the succession seems to be required by the doctrine of the Incarnation. The assumption of manhood by the pre-existent Son of GOD was *ex hypothesi* a new thing, unparalleled in human experience, seeming to require for the birth of the Incarnate Son some process that was new and unique.

That is an argument to which considerable weight must be allowed. Though the terms in which it is stated are modern, it is probable that the matter of the argument underlay the belief that our Lord was born of a Virgin. The clause in the Creed certainly affirms the belief that with Jesus something new came into the world—a new consciousness and a new power. But I distrust the argument I have stated, with its phrases 'break in the succession' and 'discontinuous', and the idea of a process of birth that was new and unique. The analogy of knowledge and theory in other departments of human observation and experience does not confirm the idea that in order to have a 'new beginning' there must be a break in the succession or discontinuity as regards the 'natural' processes at work. 'Epigenesis' and 'creative evolution' are terms which sum up the conclusions of some of the observers and thinkers who are best qualified to act as our guides in this matter; and they are terms that suggest that new creative factors may enter into the world without a breach in the continuity of the processes of 'Nature'.

And when we face the problem of personality, whether human or Divine, we are unable to feel confidence in arguments which depend on the idea that the 'personal pre-existence' of our Lord as Son of GOD was such that for a real incarnation there must be provided a human nature void of personality, which is supposed to be secured by birth from a Virgin.

We are back at the old idea that the father is the real parent of the child—giving it its 'personality' —while the mother is only the soil in which it grows, contributing to it only its substance and nature.

And the utter failure of 'orthodoxy' to attain to a real synthesis—with its two substances, two natures, and two wills (but not two 'persons')—suggests that if our doctrine of an Incarnation is to hold its place in the faith of a Christian we need to revise the terminology which is its vehicle to the mind or reason.

We reach the conclusion, accordingly, that, apart from any question of miracle or of fact, scientific theology is not helped by the traditional belief as to the way in which the Incarnation was effected. It may have been congruous with ancient conceptions of parentage and of manhood as a substance or mass or fixed quantity, which somehow had an existence *per se*, so that it could be assumed by some one who was not a man. Christian theologians of the past learned to distinguish between describing our Lord as 'Man' and speaking of Him as 'a man'. The former, they held, was right, the latter was wrong. But many of the most learned and orthodox to-day have abandoned this distinction,[1] as being one which is not really true to the evidence of the Gospels. The abandonment of this distinction seems to involve the recognition of what we must call the human personality of our Lord. We cannot find a solution in the idea of two personalities existing side by side, one of them dominant at one moment and the other at another moment; nor yet in the conception of two personalities combined and merged so as to make a third, which is neither one nor the other. But we are more ready than some of our forefathers were to recognize the 'limitation' of Divine personality and power which is implied in the very idea of Incarnation. We know that different points of

---

[1] Dr. A. J. Mason, for example, writes: "Let us frankly recognize in Him 'a man', as He calls Himself . . ."; and again: "Is not St. Paul's language [Phil. ii.] a little overdone if we follow too closely the identity of the person, instead of recognizing the wholly new position which He had taken up?" (*The Chalcedonian Doctrine of the Incarnation*, pp. 60, 61).

view are represented in the New Testament, and we are less satisfied to amalgamate them, dovetailing them all together, to form a single authoritative system of interpretation. Our faith is centred in Jesus as very 'GOD in man', but we desire to give that faith free scope and not to imprison it by presuppositions of our own or any other age. We know that whatever else He was, He was a man. He was fully a man. He had what we mean by a human personality. And our further conviction that He was also 'GOD in man', the embodiment of the Divine consciousness in man, is not incompatible with the belief that the Divine consciousness was operative in Him solely through His human consciousness, to the full extent to which a human consciousness can serve as its medium. In His case, as in no other, the Divine 'personality' expressed itself through a human 'personality': the human personality was the personality of GOD under the conditions of human life.

" Perfect Personality ", we know, " is in GOD only." So Lotze taught us afresh, though the sense of the same truth underlies a famous saying of Augustine [1] and is at least implicit in our Lord's teaching and in the Pauline and the Johannine valuations of their own experience of the personality of Jesus. It was

---

[1] Fecisti nos ad te, et inquietum est cor nostrum, donec requiescat in te.—*Confessiones* I. i.

just in His sense of utter dependence on His Father
and fellowship with men—this 'losing' of Himself
in GOD and His purposes—that His personality
found itself and came to its full expression. Each
of us, with our imperfect personalities, our incomplete
and only recurrent consciousness of our relation to
GOD and to one another, is but what Lotze called
'the pale copy' of the Personality of GOD. But
He, with His unbroken consciousness of the Father,
His realized absorption in the purpose and activity
of GOD, shewed the way in which the limits within
which we live our individual lives—the limits which
hinder us from realizing to the full our personal
potentialities—may be transcended. So He is to us
'the express image' of the Personality of GOD.[1]

We may not fully know how an individual human
personality—a genuine son of man—could become
the expression of the Divine personality, but if we are
right in admitting a human personality in our Lord
we do not derive support for our faith in Him from
a belief as to the mode of His birth which has been
the mainstay of the fiction that He was Man but
not a man. Nor does such a belief afford us any

[1] This is what the writer to the Hebrews says of Him, when we substitute the modern category of 'personality' for that of 'substance' which he used (Heb. i. 3). [The A.V. in rendering the Greek term 'person', instead of 'substance', gives it a sense which it only acquired in technical theology three centuries later, and in doing so foists upon the writer a statement that according to the ancient definitions of the Church is heretical.]

kind of explanation of the wonder which the doctrine of the Incarnation affirms.

If, then, we still retain this belief, it is as a belief out of relation to our doctrine. It is difficult to bring it into focus in the picture of our Lord and His human life and experience, and the impression He produced, on the evidence of which we found our doctrine. If the fact itself be regarded as a link in the long chain of evidence, it is not the first but the very last link, which will bear no strain, without which the chain is long enough and strong enough already—a superfluous link that hangs idly from the hand. Yet even so one need not wish to break it off. If for the Christian of one school, or at one stage of intellectual culture, it is only a last and a useless link, for others it may still be the first to catch the eye and to be clutched. The belief may still mediate for some the genuine Christian conviction and serve to stimulate the imagination and direct the will along the way of Christian thought and life.

In any case, the only form in which the doctrine of the Incarnation appears in the Apostles' Creed is the bare statement of this belief, and we are put in the paradoxical position of being obliged to profess our fundamental doctrine about our Lord in the form of a belief which appears to have no fundamental relation to the conviction we wish to affirm. There is no doubt that the clause in the Creed is intended to express this conviction—this belief in our Lord as at once GOD and man—the belief that "GOD was in Christ reconciling the world to Himself", that in Christ GOD was manifested under the *status* of a man, that in and through Him there came into human life a new Divine force, purposive, re-creative; by virtue of which human life and personality has been able to reach to a fulness of life and personality that otherwise, so far as we can judge, it might never have reached. To recite the words "conceived by the Holy Ghost, born of the Virgin Mary" in this sense is to recite them in the sense of their true religious value.[1]

[1] I am concerned to state a positive method of interpretation and not to deny interpretations of others who, intending to profess themselves whole-heartedly Christians, disciples of the Lord Jesus, find less significance in some clauses of the Creed than I do. But for my own part I cannot acquiesce in anything less than what seems to be the full doctrinal or religious sense of an old belief. And when it is suggested (1) that the words "conceived by the Holy Ghost" may be taken to mean no more than that every child born into the world is the gift of God who is the ultimate source of life, and (2) that 'Virgin Mary' may be regarded as a compound title or double name in which no definite meaning attaches to 'Virgin', as we use 'Saint' of many a canonized 'father' or 'doctor' of the Church, as a formal and complimentary title implying no judgement as to his sanctity—and so that the clause may be recited as a profession of belief that our Lord was a real historical person, born of a woman, without implying any theory like the Incarnation: I am bound to declare my conviction that such an interpretation has no kind of historical justification. It is refuted by the mere fact that in credal formulas the one word 'Virgin' originally stood alone; the personal name 'Mary' was a later addition. Human

There is yet another test by which we may judge as to the congruity of the belief before us with other Christian convictions. How is it related to our doctrine of sacraments, especially the sacrament of the Eucharist, in which Christians believe that they receive "the body and blood" of Christ?

From early times Eucharistic experience has been invoked as a test of theories of the Person of our Lord. It is, of course, in one way, a popular test, appealing to ordinary men and women, and one, therefore, that puts in the seat of judgement the emotions rather than the reason. The Incarnation and its mode, the Passion and the Resurrection—these things were ancient history to the common man; but what he received in his Communion was a matter of present and vital concern to him,[1] and the emotions must always play a large part in religious convictions and judgements as to religious values.

Yet the test suggested is also a genuinely scientific test. Our theory of the Eucharist must, if it be a reasoned theory, correspond to our theory of the

---

paternity was always intended to be excluded. The Holy Ghost and the Virgin are placed side by side as the joint authors of the person Jesus Christ. This fact is probably not as widely known as it might be. (The facts will be found detailed in Harnack's 'Appendix' to Hahn *Bibliothek der Symbole und Glaubensregeln der alten Kirche.*)

[1] I believe I owe these words to some one, but I cannot recall who it is.

Person of Christ. So, for example, one of our greatest English divines, Hooker, introduces his description of the doctrine of the Sacraments by a careful statement of the doctrine of the Person of our Lord ; and though the developement of doctrine in regard to the Eucharist does not clearly run parallel with the developement of doctrine about our Lord, and indeed seems to have other connexions, yet one form of the doctrine may have closer affinity than another with the traditional belief as to the manner of the Incarnation. In the earlier times there is, I believe, no trace of any association of the doctrine of the Eucharist with the belief in the supernatural birth. It is to establish the reality of the body born rather than the particular process of the birth that the analogy of Eucharistic belief was used in the second century ; as it was real bread that was received, so it was a real body that was born. It was not, as some 'heretics' taught, a phantom body that the Word of GOD assumed, but a body as real as the Eucharistic bread which is able to nourish our bodies. No Christian could tolerate the idea that the bread of the Eucharist was an illusion ; nor, therefore, was Christ's body illusory. The argument in no way depends on belief in the miraculous conception, but only on the belief that the real bread was a vehicle of a supernatural power of life.

In the belief that the bread becomes the life-giving body of Christ, there is no doubt already latent the germ of a conception that was to have a profound influence in later times—the conception that the actual body of Jesus in His life on earth was so transmuted to a Divine dignity by His Divine personality within it that it was not subject to the ordinary affections and 'laws' of ordinary bodies. This conception is, indeed, inherent in the Gospel stories of His walking on water and suddenly vanishing out of the midst of a crowd. But "the line had to be drawn somewhere", and in the earlier days, when there was danger that the whole historical basis and framework of the new Religion might suffer dissolution, the main body of Churchmen were chiefly concerned to lay stress on the fact that the Redeemer was really man, and it was in this interest that the analogy of Eucharistic belief was used.[1] There was no question in dispute as to the reality of His Godhead or as to the superhuman potency of the Eucharist, so reference was not called for to the mode of the Incarnation. And later on analogy was found between the Eucharistic 'body'

---

[1] If there is any historical relation, by way of cause and effect, between Eucharistic doctrine and the conception referred to above, I suspect it is a case of the doctrine of our Lord's Person (as regards His manhood) being affected by prevalent beliefs as to the change which the bread in the Eucharist underwent. It might thus be an illustration of the way in which Theology has been made by ideas working upwards from below. Yet docetic conceptions of our Lord's manhood have been present in the Church from the Apostolic age to our own day.

and the glorified body of the ascended Lord, rather than the body as it was on earth.

In the latter part of the fourth century, however, Ambrose[1] definitely bases his teaching about the Sacrament on the Miraculous Birth. "The body which we make" in the Eucharist is, he says, the body born of the Virgin. It is not, of course, the natural order of experience that is seen in the Sacrament of the body of Christ; but how could that be expected when the birth itself was outside the natural order of experience? Yet he lays stress on the character of the food obtained in the Sacrament as spiritual and not material; it is the spiritual 'body' of Christ that is received: and he insists that the flesh of Christ was real flesh. The analogy between the sacramental body and the actual body born of the Virgin, therefore, fails. The real analogy which he has in mind is between the Incarnation and the Sacrament as both alike transcending the natural order and both alike being manifestations of 'the excellency of grace'. He does not mean that the body born of the Virgin was other than a human body, whereas he does teach that the bread was transformed by consecration so as to become a spiritual body. It is not the manner of the birth

---

[1] I do not recall any earlier reference, but it is the type of theory rather than the date of its origin with which we are concerned. Ambrose was not an original thinker and he probably took his *rationale* of the Eucharist from some one else.

that matters for his argument, but the fact of the Incarnation—the fact that in the 'making' of the whole personality of Jesus Christ, as in the 'making' of the Sacrament, a power transcending natural experience was at work.

For a theory of the Sacrament such as 'transubstantiation' as it is popularly understood, or even Gregory of Nyssa's 'transformation' which Ambrose possibly had in mind in his own exposition, support might be derived from the belief that our Lord's actual body was produced in some miraculous way. The two beliefs would certainly be congruous the one with the other, though neither can be said to require or to lead logically to the other.

But a doctrine of the Sacrament which insists on its supernatural character and potency, while leaving the exact manner of the process undefined, would be congruous with a doctrine of the Incarnation which, fully recognizing the supernatural character and potency of the personality of Jesus, yet had no theory as to the manner of the process by which the Incarnation was effected.

And a doctrine of the Sacrament which repudiated the theory of transubstantiation, as popularly understood, and insisted that the bread and the wine, produced by the ordinary intelligence of man applied to the ordinary products of Nature, remained bread and wine, while indefinably affected by association and use so as to become the expression of Divine potency, the very organ of the personality of Christ, and the vehicles of an experience transcending the common order of experience : such a doctrine of the Sacrament as this would be congruous with a doctrine of the Incarnation which, while not professing to have any explanation to offer of the How, and basing itself on such evidence as is described earlier in this enquiry, found in a man naturally born a supernatural character and potency, and recognized in Him, in His own recorded experience on earth and in the experiences of others in regard to Him, the manifestation of the personality of GOD.

Both these doctrines would be congruous with each other. And if GOD be recognized as in any true sense immanent in Nature and in Man—or if Nature and Man be regarded rather as having their being and existence in GOD ; if Nature is a revelation of the power and wisdom and attributes of GOD, and if human personality is a reflexion in part of the Personality of GOD so that GOD is the underlying or central reality of every human personality, then such doctrines of the Sacraments and the Incarnation, while they would indeed pourtray a process or processes transcending the natural order of experience, would yet represent them as only summary and supreme examples of the ordinary relation between GOD and Nature and Man—

instances, if the expression may be allowed, of the ordinary and regular action of GOD raised to its highest power. What we call the 'sacramental' conception of the Universe, of Nature, and of Life elicits a rare response from reason, imagination, and will. May we not trust it more fully?

'Materialistic' and 'magical' are terms which we may well be loth to use of any belief of Christians which has helped them to lead Christian lives in the midst of surroundings material and mysterious, suggesting secrets, the discovery of which would place untold resources at their disposal, and powers which can be made to do their will. There is, too, a 'mechanical' element in every expression of faith and every institution by which the lives of men are fashioned and controlled. But there is upward progress of individuals and of races in ideas of Religion as in other things; and there is reaction and retrogression, sometimes through lack of courage to follow up fresh knowledge where it seems to lead. 'Materialistic' and 'magical' are terms that may be used properly of some conceptions of the Incarnation and the Sacraments, at all events as chronological notes defining the stage in this progress of Religion at which the individual or the society is at the moment. The same genuine religious conviction or faith may be apprehended and expressed in either a 'magical' or a 'spiritual' form. Such antitheses are as necessary for the definition of thought as are the antitheses 'natural and supernatural', 'human and Divine': whether they express ultimate realities or not, they express what is true in our experience, while we 'know in part'. In like manner, the 'immanence' of GOD in Nature and His 'transcendence' of Nature are antithetical truths which religious experience owns and requires for its interpretation of itself. That is to say, religious experience recognizes the continuous action of GOD in natural processes — in the whole world-process, and yet nevertheless finds itself compelled to the conviction that He also transcends these processes. It is not, however, forced to the conclusion that He ever invades or counteracts them in such a way as to overthrow the natural order, which is for Religion not only the expression of His will, but also the means to the ultimate fulfilment of His purpose.

The doctrine of the Sacrament which I have indicated above is entirely congruous with the formularies of the Church of England. And when we reason in terms of personality rather than of substance, the doctrine of the Incarnation which is congruous with this doctrine of the Sacrament may be found to be not out of harmony with the faith of a Christian according to the religious construction of the Creed.

NOTE

I have stated above my conviction that the belief in our Lord's birth from a virgin is not implied in any of the passages in the Epistles of St. Paul and the Johannine writings in which some students have discovered it. The following are the passages.

(1) Gal. iv. 4, "God sent forth his son, γενόμενον ἐκ γυναικός, γενόμενον ὑπὸ νόμον." The same Greek word is used in both clauses and we have no single English word to represent it well, especially as its sense is really determined in the two clauses by the two different prepositional phrases. The first clause points to origination, the latter to condition, of life in the world. As regards the first clause, which alone concerns us, either the A.V. 'made of a woman', or the R.V. 'born of a woman', gives the sense nearly enough. St. Paul's point is that God sent forth His Son into the world as man to be subject to the conditions to which men were subject. He underwent the process of human birth, was 'born of woman'. St. Paul used the only expression he could naturally have used: we do not speak of birth from a man.

To say, as was said by Zahn (referred to by A. E. Burn, *The Apostles' Creed*, p. 73), that "he only mentions the mother when, for the purpose of his argument, it would be more to the point to mention a Jewish father", is to misunderstand the argument and to ignore the fact that the phrase 'of a woman' (so far as it goes) implies an ordinary human birth, and that if St. Paul had intended anything else here he could have said 'of a virgin'— though it is true that his argument would have been seriously weakened by the suggestion that the conditions of our Lord's entrance on human life were fundamentally different from those of the men whose experience he came to share. The argument, so far as it goes, is evidence rather that our Lord's birth from a virgin mother was not part of St. Paul's belief about Him.

(2) 1 Tim. ii. 15, σωθήσεται δὲ διὰ τῆς τεκνογονίας, "she shall be brought safe through her child-bearing".

I have no doubt that the A.V. is substantially right in its rendering "she shall be saved in child-bearing". The reference in the preceding verses is to the account of creation, the Fall, and the Curse in Genesis iii., the blame being put on the woman. (The whole account, of course, comes to us through the medium of men and reflects this masculine medium and the Oriental conception of the relative position of the two sexes, from which St. Paul himself was not entirely freed by his Christian ideals. The woman's story might have been different.) For σωθῆναι διὰ . . . cf. 1 Cor. iii. 15, 1 Pet. iii. 20. It is an instance of the well-recognized idiomatic use of the preposition in its 'local' sense — 'passing through', 'in a state of'. The verb τεκνογονεῖν and its cognates are 'classical' and no doubt were in ordinary use.

The τεκνογονία is the state in which the penalty pronounced on the woman for her share in the Fall takes effect, and women are promised a safe passage through it "if they continue in faith and love and holiness with sobriety".

It is impossible that, in such a context as this at all events, St. Paul could have used the phrase ἡ τεκνογονία as a technical term for the Incarnation, or with any reference to the birth of our Lord. If he could have done so, the term would in no way suggest any special mode of birth and could have no kind of reference to the virginity of the mother.

(3) 1 Cor. xv. 45 f.—I am not concerned to argue that St. Paul's conception of our Lord's personality definitely excludes the idea of a miraculous birth. But I can find no implicit

reference to such a mode of birth in his teaching about our Lord as the 'last Adam', the 'second man', 'from heaven'. That teaching may imply something like a Platonic (or 'Egyptian') conception of the ideal Man of the whole race reserved 'in heaven' till the moment of his manifestation on earth, but for that manifestation a human birth is, by St. Paul at any rate, presupposed; and there is no evidence that St. Paul would have required as a background for his conception belief in a birth from a virgin mother.

(4) John i. 12, 13, "But as many as received him, to them he gave the right to become children of GOD; even to them that believe on his name: who were born (begotten) not of blood, nor of the will of the flesh, nor of the will of man, but of GOD".

The second part of this passage (*v.* 13) is clearly explanatory of the phrases of the first part—"as many as received him", "children of GOD", and "that believe on his name". The process described is the supernatural process of faith, which the spirit of GOD originates, by which men naturally born undergo a second birth and become "children of GOD". They are "begotten of GOD" —a thought and a phrase which dominates the First Epistle of St. John.

The meaning of the passage is certain, and no editors of the text have any doubt of its being right. But a variant "who was born", instead of "who were born", was current in the second century, and was known to Justin, Irenaeus, and Tertullian. As regards the transmission of the text the singular might easily have arisen accidentally (by unconscious adaptation on the scribe's part) from the personal pronoun in the singular which immediately precedes it, and to a copyist who believed in the miraculous birth of our Lord it would be an almost mechanical correction, though not an intelligent one. The whole weight of MS. evidence is against the reading, and it has no claim to be considered authentic.

But, accepting the received text, it has been argued that the supernatural birth of the Logos is here presupposed as a kind of pattern or model of the birth of the children of GOD (W. C. Allen, *Interpreter*, October 1905): "As He was born into the world by supernatural conception, not through the process of human generation, so they were born out of the world into the higher life by a spiritual process, symbolized indeed by generation, but transcending it" (p. 57 f.). A suggestion so subtle as this seems to me to elude the possibility of refutation. But I cannot see how the miraculous process of the *physical* birth of our Lord could seem analogous to the supernatural process of the *spiritual* regeneration of men who were born by a natural process. The supernatural origin of a body seems to offer no parallel to the process by which men who are born "of blood" "of the will of the flesh" and of the will of man can become "children of GOD".

The passage as it stands does not offer us any indication of belief on the writer's part in the birth of our Lord without a human father.

(5) Revelation xii.—The woman "arrayed with the sun" who "brought forth a man child" is a figure derived from Babylonian mythology. Its incorporation in this book and its application to the mother of the Messiah has no reference to the belief in the miraculous birth of our Lord. It is the Jewish Church who is the Mother, and the writer calls her 'woman' not 'virgin'.

These, I believe, are the only passages in the writings of St. Paul and St. John in which microscopic scrutiny of the text has detected reference to the traditional belief. No one, I venture to say, would find evidence of the belief in any of these passages if he was not determined to find it somewhere in these groups of writings, and the time for defending Christian doctrine by exegesis of Scripture which is either clearly wrong or purely speculative is surely past. We cannot to-day hope to substantiate any alleged fact in our Lord's life, or any Christian doctrine, unless we can justify it by the kind of evidence or reasoning that is appropriate to the truth it is to establish. We reject the 'argument from silence' when it is used against traditional beliefs. But the price we pay for this limitation of negative arguments is obvious. We cannot draw positive arguments from passages which have no evident bearing on the question at issue.[1]

[1] In an article in *The Expositor* (October 1918), published as these pages leave me, Professor J. H. Michael, of Toronto, gives strong reasons for thinking that the origin of the passage John i. 12, 13 is to be found in the Sophia-hymn (Wisdom of Solomon, vii.), and further support to the view that belief in 'the Virgin Birth' does not accord with the Logos conception of the Gospel and was not held by its author.

V

"SUFFERED UNDER PONTIUS PILATE, WAS CRUCIFIED, DEAD, AND BURIED, HE DESCENDED INTO HELL"

IT has been said that this is the only purely historical statement in the Creed, one which can be verified as securely as any statement about events in the past. That may be true of the first part of the statement, and the name of the Roman Governor no doubt was intended to guarantee its historical character and to date the event in accordance with ancient custom, our own legal usage, and common habit to-day in our colonies where 'governors' still exist. But no one could maintain that the final clause of the statement was historical in the same sense, though there is no reason to suppose that when it was inserted in the Creed it was intended to be taken less literally or regarded as less historical than the clauses as to the Death and Burial.

It is also said that no doctrine of atonement is expressed in the Apostles' Creed in direct connexion with the death of our Lord, and indeed that there is only one saying recorded in the Synoptic Gospels which definitely assigns to His death redemptive value—" The Son of man . . . came . . . to give his life a ransom for many" (Mark x. 45, Matt. xx. 28). The idea of atonement in the popular sense of the word was certainly not prominent in our Lord's mind, though the absorbing purpose of His life was to bring all men to the consciousness of the Fatherhood and righteousness of GOD which He Himself possessed. Yet it is clear that before the end of His life He had come to believe that a violent death at the hands of the rulers of the people was probably His fate, and that only by such a death could GOD'S purpose be accomplished and the Kingdom come. His later teaching is permeated with the conviction that the destiny of the Son of Man was to suffer greatly, and that in the process of establishing the new order in the world His own death would be of paramount influence.

So as soon as His earliest disciples had adapted their natural conceptions of the Redeemer of Israel to the facts of their actual experience, they began to see unique significance in the death on the Cross. Christ as crucified, though to Jews a stumbling-block and to Gentiles folly, was the centre of the good news St. Paul preached—not by any means the whole of it, but the supreme secret, the amazing paradox of the Divine economy. And when in the Creed belief in Christ crucified is declared, it is not a mere statement of belief in a historical event that is made, but a profession of faith in a process of real redemption of mankind, in the working out of which the Death on the Cross was an integral factor.

When Ignatius wrote (*Ad Eph.* 19) of the three secrets which were wrought in GOD'S silence and hidden from the Devil, though now to be shouted out aloud—Mary's virginity, her child-bearing, and the death of the Lord—he did not mean the fact of the death, but its significance. The 'death of the Lord' meant the atonement, the restoration, the regeneration, however we describe it. It meant, that is, the Christian interpretation of the whole complex of experiences connected with the Death.

So the statement in the Creed is simple enough; but in its place in the Creed its value and its significance is conditioned and determined by the intention of the Creed as a whole. In their particular setting the words imply a spiritual conviction and a process unique in character. When we use them as our own profession of faith we declare our belief that the death of Jesus was a fact of eternal moment in the history of the human race. In the Eastern Creed, by the addition of the words "who for us men and for our salvation . . . came down from heaven" and "for us" after "was crucified", the personal and spiritual valuation of the clause is actually expressed; but the shorter and colder Western form means as much. The personal debt and the personal tie to Jesus is implied throughout the Creed.

No 'theory of the atonement' is defined : no theory of atonement has ever been defined as an article of the Creed by the Church. How the death of Christ avails—the death which is only the culminating point in His experiences as man, the culminating point in the Passion of His whole life on earth ; what exact place it occupies in the whole of GOD'S purposes or in the whole doctrine of the Incarnation and of the Church and the Sacraments—these are questions which have often been discussed and may well continue to be discussed. In the New Testament itself we have from different writers, as is natural, different points of view expressed, corresponding to their various temperaments and antecedents and experience : here one metaphor and there another. We can choose the one which is congruous with our own temperament without denying the validity of others. And, throughout the centuries since, elaborate theories have been framed to correspond with the philosophical or political or social conditions and interests of successive ages, and even of different classes of the community. We can be, for example, imperialistic or absolutist, or feudal or monarchical, or constitutionalist or democratic, in our theory of the atonement as we are in our theory of GOD, or our theory of the State. We can lay chief stress on either the representative or the vicarious character of the atonement, provided always that we do not concentrate our minds on one of these aspects of it to the exclusion of the other. If we regard it chiefly as something done for us, we may not forget that it is also something done in us and that it leaves us much to do for ourselves. We can think of it mainly as a unique event in the history of our race, creative of a new consciousness in men and a new relation to GOD, or mainly as a supreme example of a process which, when once it is realized, all human experience attests as being of immemorial, eternal potency. The Creed leaves all such questions open.

But even its bare words imply something as to the method; for they do not stand alone and cannot be taken apart from the statement of belief in the Incarnation which precedes them and of belief in the Resurrection which follows them. It is faith in the Person who died as being "the only Son of GOD" and as risen again from the dead, that gives the criterion for the valuation of the Death itself, and constitutes it for us the supreme proof not only that GOD is love but also that the way to Life lies through the uttermost sacrifice of self: " He that will lose his life shall find it." Life comes by sacrifice and lives by service; it is perpetually re-created by the very act of laying it down. We profess our acceptance of this law of life, with all that it involves, when we profess belief in the suffering and death of Jesus.

There is no need to dwell longer on this clause of the Creed. It is followed by one the meaning and religious value of which is less obvious, which therefore needs to be more fully considered.

"He descended into Hell." No ingenuity can disguise the fact that in its literal sense this clause expresses a belief which Christians do not hold to-day. It is not simply a case of words having lost their original sense and come to be mere figures of speech, or of an archaic view of the universe such as is reflected in other clauses of the Creed. 'Hell' does not represent to English ears merely the state of the dead, nor did 'Hades' and 'the infernal regions' represent, in Greek and Latin respectively, merely the state of the dead to those who first inserted the clause in Creeds. The vast majority of Christians who have used the Apostles' Creed as the statement of their own beliefs have understood that our Lord after death actually passed to the place where the Devil rules over the lost, or 'damned', or 'the spirits which were detained in prison'; and they have not always understood that He went there as the Conqueror of death and the Devil.[1] More

[1] The cry of desolation from the Cross—the only cry known to the author of the earliest gospel and apparently to the author of the gospel according to St. Matthew—is evidence of the extent to which our Lord

particularly as the mediaeval conception of the event has become unfamiliar, the clause has been a stumbling-block, and it has been evacuated of much of its religious meaning. It certainly means something more than 'experienced the condition of death' which has already been declared of Him in the Creed. The process of retranslation of old beliefs is always difficult; and when Ptolemaic ideas as well as phraseology have to be abandoned, there is danger that the spiritual reality which the idea once represented may fail to obtain recognition. This is peculiarly the case with regard to the belief in our Lord's descent into Hell, and this clause of the Creed offers an excellent criterion of the value of the method of interpretation we are following in recovering the real affirmations of faith—the real religious convictions—of a Christian, out of the wreckage of the beliefs in which they were encased. It is worth while to review the history of this clause in some detail.

---

shared in the most poignant of all human experiences which can befall the soul; and Calvin, for example, insisted on taking the Descent into Hell as meaning that our Lord really bore in His soul the full experience of the tortures of condemned and ruined man (*Inst.* II. xvi. 10). In this view, however, he went far outside the primitive conception.

Yet the full manifestation of the love of GOD seems to require participation in the extremest sufferings of man, and at an earlier stage in His life the baptism of Jesus at the hands of John implies His own consciousness of the need of repentance and so the sense of sin— though later Christian thought could not tolerate this idea and converted what was surely one of our Lord's deepest human experiences into a merely outward and formal ceremony performed for the sake of example to others.

The origin of the belief in the Descent is obscure. Some scholars have traced it to mythological influences, and if we agree with the latest investigator of the belief[1] that it is a primitive Christian idea which has no relation whatever with the alleged parallels of other religions, yet mythological influences seem certainly to have affected details of the belief in its later stages. The question must have presented itself, Where was Jesus in the interval between His Death and the Resurrection?

The mediaeval belief expressed by the phrase 'the Harrowing of Hell', and familiar to us from pictures, represents our Lord in the interval between His Death and Resurrection as going down to Hades, overcoming the Devil, destroying the power of Hell, and releasing the Old Testament saints. Theologians, it is true, declared that it was not to Hell itself that He descended, not to the very *infernus damnatorum*, but to the forecourt, the *limbus*, the 'belt' or 'fringe' of Hell, where the Old Testament fathers dwelt. But this distinction, like some other theological distinctions, was too subtle to win wide currency, and many of the pictures have as their scene Satan's fortress, even the jaws of Hell; and the victory over the Devil

[1] F. Loofs, "Christ's Descent into Hell", in *Transactions of the Third International Congress of the History of Religions*, Oxford, 1908, vol. ii. pp. 290 ff. This article, with Pearson's in his *Exposition of the Creed*, furnishes all the evidence available.

is a prominent feature in the work of releasing the Saints.[1]

The mediaeval belief no doubt arose from the so-called *Gospel of Nicodemus*, which was perhaps composed in the fourth century and was widespread in later times. It contains a vivid account of the Descent into Hades, the joy of the Old Testament saints, the chaining of the Devil (who tried to imprison Christ) and his being thrust into Tartarus, the place of torment. But the imaginative author of the *Gospel of Nicodemus* was not the originator of the belief itself: he only gave it dramatic expression and developement.

In the middle of the second century Justin (*Dial.* 72) knows, as a prophecy of Jeremiah, which he says the Jews have cut out of the text, these words: "The Lord, the GOD (*or* the Holy One) of Israel, remembered his dead who were asleep in the earth which was their tomb, and he descended to

---

[1] Of these pictures Luther himself declared, "I am pleased with what is painted: that Christ descends with banner in hand, comes to hell, smites the devil and expels him, storms hell and rescues His own"; "Thus the people would be led to believe that Christ has released us from hell." And the Lutheran profession of faith, the *Formula Concordiae*, embodies the same conception. The third of the Thirty-nine Articles of the Church of England says no more than that "it is to be believed that [Christ] went down into Hell", the explanations and the Scriptural proof which had been appended in the article as drawn up in 1553 being omitted at the revision in Elizabeth's reign, probably in view of differences of opinion among the Reformers as to more than the fact itself.

them to preach to them his salvation." With the variation 'his saints' for 'his dead', and adding 'in order to save them', Irenaeus cites this prophecy no fewer than six times (*e.g. Adv. Haer.* iii. 20. 4 Mass., vol. ii. p. 108 Harvey, Ἀπόδειξις § 78). A Descent of Christ that had in view primarily the salvation of the Old Testament saints was thus clearly the belief of Justin and Irenaeus, and the same belief is found in Tertullian (*De Anima* 7, 55), Clement of Alexandria (*Strom.* vi. 6. Migne ix. 265), and even Origen (*Contr. Cels.* ii. 43), and it is implied in Marcion (see Iren. *Adv. Haer.* i. 27. 3—Harvey vol. i. p. 218).

In this form of the belief,[1] current in the middle of the second century, the purpose of the descent is to carry the good news of the fulfilment of the hope of Israel to those who had believed under the old covenant: to shew that GOD is not unmindful of His own, and that faith will be rewarded.

The passages 1 Pet. iii. 19 and iv. 6 probably have nothing to do with the Descent,[2] and in any case have nothing in common with this conception of its purpose. They are not cited by the early writers in support of their belief, nor can it be traced to the New Testament.

[1] Iren. iv. 27. 2 (H. ii. 241) cites one of the presbyters (*i.e.* older Christians of his country) as authority—so it probably originated in Asia Minor.

[2] Similarly Eph. iv. 9 means 'this earth of ours' contrasted with the heavens above, and refers to the 'coming down' in the Incarnation: but it may have been misunderstood early as it has been later.

HE DESCENDED INTO HELL

The earliest reference to the belief is perhaps in Ignatius (*Ad Magn.* ix.): "The prophets who were his disciples in spirit (*or* join with the following words 'by the spirit') expected him as teacher; and therefore he whom they justly (rightly) awaited, when he came (παρών, *or* came and) raised them from the dead." We cannot be confident that Ignatius shews here any idea of a Descent of our Lord to the abode of the dead (παρών seems rather to suggest His coming to earth): but there is a clear conception of the bestowal of new life on the faithful of old, who had looked for Him, as a result of His coming (to be 'raised from the dead' to Ignatius probably means to enter on eternal life, as he hoped himself to 'attain unto GOD'). And it is possible that from this seed-thought, in connexion with the disputed prophecy, the idea, which we find later among writers who had connexion with Asia Minor, grew up.

It does not appear to have been current in Rome in the time of Hermas (*i.e. c.* 140), as he (*Sim.* ix. 16. 5) represents the Old Testament saints as becoming acquainted with the name of the Son of GOD through the preaching of the apostles (not Christ) in Hades. It could not, therefore, have been a generally current belief.[1]

[1] Dr. Loofs indeed finds traces of it in Rev. i. 18; John viii. 56, "Your father Abraham rejoiced to see my day; *and he saw it and was glad*" (*sc.* at the Descent: this interpretation is given also by the Gnostic Theodotus, Clem. *excerpta ex Theod.* 18, Migne ix. 666)—of

All that is certainly primitive is the belief that Christ after His death, like all the dead, 'descended' into the realm of the dead (*i.e.* Sheol or Hades). Every Jew must have believed this.[1] What Christians of the apostolic age believed to be the condition after death of those who had believed in Christ in this life we cannot say with certainty. St. Paul was confident that death itself could not separate him from the love of Christ (Rom. viii. 38 f.) and, though this passage and others of similar tone are mystic rather than dogmatic, John xi. 26 reflects the belief that believers in Christ would not be held in death (" every one that liveth and believeth in me shall never die "). Reverence for the patriarchs and prophets, who by anticipation believed in the coming Messiah, would surely suggest the belief that they too were released from the state in which they were before the coming of Christ annulled the power of death. We must at all events bear this belief in mind in considering the meaning of the doctrine of the Descent in the Creed.

Clauses to this effect are first found in Creeds

---

course a strong anachronism if so interpreted; Matt. xxvii. 51 f., "an incomplete and coarse reminiscence" (the bodies of saints arising . . .); and notably Heb. xi. 39 f., xii. 22 f. (cf. ix. 8).

[1] Acts ii. 31 " Nor was he left in Hades "; Rom. x. 7 " Who will go down into the abyss? that is to bring Christ up from the dead"; Matt. xii. 40 " So shall the Son of man be in the heart of the earth three days and three nights "; and probably Luke xxiii. 43 " This day thou shalt be with me in Paradise ".

after the middle of the fourth century (*e.g.* the Creed drawn up in 359 at the synod of Sirmium, revised at Nice, in Thrace, and again at Constantinople, 359-360)—"who also went down into the nether world (τὰ καταχθόνια), and when the gate-keepers of Hades saw him they shuddered",[1] *or* "at whom Hades himself was affrighted". The actual clause of our Creed first had a place in the Creed of Aquileia on which Rufinus commented in 399. Rufinus does not know its origin, but he interprets it as explanatory of the words 'was buried'. No such clause seems to have been in the Creed of Cyril of Jerusalem (*c.* 350), but in his catechetical lectures on the Creed he refers several times to the Descent, and includes it in his list of 'things to be believed' as explanatory of the clause on the Burial (*e.g. Cat.* iv. 11, 12). It is not the Death with which either of these early exponents of the Creed connect it, but the Burial; and the dramatic language of the Greek Creeds just cited shews that a definite and conscious experience after death was intended to be understood.

Moreover, against Apollinaris, who denied that our Lord had a human rational soul, the belief in the Descent was constantly appealed to as evidence of our Lord's complete manhood by orthodox writers

---

[1] There is a reference to Job xxxviii. 17 LXX. : "Did the gate-keepers of Hades shudder when they saw thee?"

in the fourth century and later, and it has a place in the Athanasian Creed which is specially concerned to contradict all theories of an Apollinarian tendency. The strength of the argument at this time of course depended on the belief that the Descent into Hell was as real an event, as 'historical' an incident, as the Birth, the Crucifixion, or the Burial.

Thus, so far as ancient testimony goes, we may indeed say that the primary intention of the clause in the Creed is to insist that our Lord passed through all human experiences, that He not only died a real death and was buried, but that while His Body lay in the tomb, He Himself passed into the place in which all human beings are when Death separates them from the earthly body. And we may go further and say that in doing this He hallowed the state after Death as He hallowed each age of man by passing through it in His life, and brought hope and comfort to mourners, and courage and confidence to men when the hour of death approaches for themselves:—they need not fear to go where He went. Nothing forbids this further interpretation of the clause. And though we know that it meant much more to Christians of old, much that we can no longer believe, we may describe all that as the embroidery of the main belief and take our stand on the facts that the earliest commentators on the Creed interpret the clause as we have seen, and that the mediaeval ideas of Hell and limbo, which are still current among many Christians, are of pagan rather than Christian origin. We are not bound to-day by Virgil's or Dante's description of the state of the dead; and the few passages in Scripture which can reasonably be interpreted as in any way referring to our Lord's state or actions in the interval between His Death on the Cross and His appearances to the disciples cannot bear the structure which either early or mediaeval imagination reared in connexion with belief in our Lord's descent into Hades.

But intellectual sincerity demands that we should recognize how thoroughly we have stripped off the factual cover of the belief. And yet, here, too, when we strip off the embroidery, and ask what is the essential element in the belief which underlies the clause, we find that the early beliefs which were expressed in these archaic forms have permanent religious values. They declare more clearly than any other article in the Apostles' Creed the universality of the Gospel. The conquest of Death was achieved by Christ not for Himself alone, but for all who have faith in Him. That is what the symbolism of the Banner and the thrusting of the Devil into Tartarus means. If after this life there is still a state preceding Resurrection, it is one over which the

Devil does not rule. This conception certainly has full Scriptural authority and permanent religious value.

And the conception of the release of the Jewish saints, limited by the Jewish horizon in regard to revelation as it is, expresses essentially the same idea as the λόγος σπερματικός of Justin. As Justin claims that all who, before the Incarnation of the Logos, lived with logos (reason) were partakers of the Logos—that Socrates, for example, should rank as a Christian—so the belief that our Lord preached salvation to the Jewish saints stands for the conception of the absoluteness of Christianity—of the eternal life-giving power of the Spirit of Christ, which has no limits of time, but is the source of all that is good and true in all ages among all peoples.

The ideas, then, which the clause conveys to us, when historically examined and construed in its religious sense, are these: the full manhood and human experiences of Christ, the idea of an 'intermediate state' after death, the hallowing of the state of the faithful departed, the universality and absoluteness of the Gospel: and they are no mean part of the common Christian Faith.

'THE INTERMEDIATE STATE'

Before we go on to the next clause of the Creed, there is a belief, closely connected with the belief in our Lord's Descent into Hell, which has had so large a place in Christian faith and practice and is so intimately associated with the Christian outlook on life, that it cannot be passed over in silence. It has to do with the state immediately following death. What is the condition, according to the faith of a Christian, of those "who sleep in Christ"?

It appears to have been the current belief among Jews in the time of our Lord that the faithful Israelite after death had to make his way through subterranean passages and caverns till he reached the Valley of Jehoshaphat, where with the Patriarchs he must wait for the general Resurrection. This journey, attended by difficulties and dangers, would take eleven months; and all that time the eldest son of the deceased, his first-born, was bound to recite each day a prayer that the Almighty would remember and look favourably on His servant. Many Jews, I am informed, recite this prayer for a year, though they may not know or share the belief on which it was based; and even Jews who observe few other of the ancient customs of their race will still recite the prayer once a year, on the anniversary of a parent's death. It may reasonably be assumed that the first Jewish Christians would maintain the custom, even if their conception of the state of the departed was modified. That Christians did not believe that Death was immediately succeeded by entrance on eternal life is clearly shewn by St. Paul's treatment of the perplexity of the Thessalonian Christians as to the fortunes of their friends who had already passed away since becoming Christians. St. Paul assumes that they are in a state of existence from which they must be aroused and summoned to share in the reign of Christ upon earth when He comes again to establish His Kingdom. They are not in 'heaven'. St. Paul's mystic conception of union with Christ which death could not break has been referred to above. But on the only occasion on which, so far as we know, he was called upon to give direct and definite teaching on the question of the state of the departed faithful, he speaks in no uncertain tone. There is a stage for souls to pass through between this life and the life of the Kingdom of GOD. But in that stage the Christian is not separated from the love of Christ: that is the ground of his confidence and the consolation of those who mourn him here. The saying to the penitent robber on the Cross (recorded by St. Luke xxiii. 43)—he should be with the Lord of the Kingdom, not in the Kingdom itself, but in its anteroom—seems to be intended as a special encouragement to the penitent which cannot rightly be used as evidence in general. Nor can much stress be laid on any details of the parable of the Rich Man and Lazarus (Luke xvi.); we cannot rightly draw from it any confirmation of theories as to the state of the departed. The subject of the parable was the unconscious selfishness of the rich and their neglect of the claims of the poor around them, and the ethical teaching was simply driven home by an illustration from current conceptions of the future life; its standards are not those of this life: let the world take warning.

Again we are driven back to the one sure guide, our Lord's own experiences, rather than precarious inferences from the ideas of the Jews of the time which He used to illustrate His teaching. He Himself passed through an 'intermediate state', before He entered on or resumed the heavenly state. In the language of Scripture, not till the third day did He 'rise' again; not till after a further interval of forty days did He 'ascend' (*or* was He 'taken up') into heaven. And all the period was according to Christian tradition a time of spiritual activity wider in its range than the time of earthly life; a time during which surely the learning from the things which He experienced went on, and the human personality was still further perfected, becoming a more complete expression of the Divine personality in its fulness.

And if "the Son of man" went through that course, a similar experience may be expected to await all the sons of men, and something like "some place of instruction, and as it were a class-room or school of souls", of which Origen thought (*De Princ.* ii. ch. xi. § 6), would represent their state, and prayer for them by those still living in the world would be as great an aid to them as it was while they were here. We have seen that we can only speak of probabilities as to the custom of the first Christians. Positive evidence is lacking till after the middle of the second century: but as regards the most intimate private practice of Christians nearly all evidence is lacking till much later times. Early in the third century we know that the Eucharist itself was offered for the faithful departed, and before the end of the same century intercession for the dead seems to have been everywhere a familiar feature of the liturgy.[1] In the course of time, ideas which have no necessary connexion with the custom were associated with it, and because those subsidiary ideas were rejected by some branches of the Church in the sixteenth century, the custom itself, among members of those branches of the Church, fell into abeyance not only in the public liturgy, but even to a large extent in private practice. What the loss has been to the departed no one can estimate. The loss to the living, to those left in the world, may be partly gauged by the general inability to realize the continuity of human life before and after death. The practice of prayer for the departed, an absolute necessity to some, in some cases, is for all a chief means of realizing the Christian faith in the life of the world to come.

---

[1] See the evidence collected by Dr. Swete, *Journal of Theological Studies* vol. viii. pp. 500 ff.

VI

"THE THIRD DAY HE ROSE AGAIN FROM THE DEAD, HE ASCENDED INTO HEAVEN, AND SITTETH ON THE RIGHT HAND OF GOD THE FATHER ALMIGHTY; FROM THENCE HE SHALL COME TO JUDGE THE QUICK AND THE DEAD"

No short summary of the evidence with regard to the Resurrection is possible, but the belief undoubtedly rests on actual experiences of those who had known and been with our Lord during His life on earth. What was the exact nature of those experiences we are not able to determine. We only know that they were of such a kind as to convince men and women that Jesus was alive again and able to convey the sense of His living presence to them. Their interpretation of these experiences is contained in the Gospels in the narratives of the appearances of our Lord, and these narratives all imply the resuscitation to life of the Body that died. They also seem to imply that the 'body' could be materialized or dematerialized at will. There can be no doubt that the clause in the Creed also implies this belief in the re-animation of the body—a belief which is stated fully in detail in the fourth of the Thirty-nine Articles of the Church of England.[1] But our Article sums up the belief in a more general phrase when it speaks of "all things appertaining to the perfection of man's nature".

That is perhaps one of the happiest phrases in a series of Articles composed at a time when religious convictions were often too sharply defined. It expresses the constant faith of the Church in contrast with all theories of the other world and the afterlife which conceive of men as being less 'men' in it than they were in this life, mere shadows of themselves, pale 'disembodied' ghosts; or, again, in contrast with the widespread and in some ways attractive belief that only the soul, the highest and noblest part, of a man survived the death of the body—a belief that at all events encouraged the cultivation in this life of what were regarded as the highest capacities of the soul. Against such ideas of immortality as these the traditional belief in the

[1] "Christ did truly rise again from death, and took again his body, with flesh, bones, and all things appertaining to the perfection of Man's nature; wherewith he ascended into Heaven, and there sitteth, until he return to judge all Men at the last day."

Resurrection of Jesus stands for the conviction that it was the whole man, the whole personality, all that had gone to make Him what He was in this life, that survived the Crucifixion and the Burial, or 'rose' or 'was raised' again. The individual personality was not lost or dissipated or absorbed in something greater than itself; it was all there, freed, as we say, from some of its earthly limitations, but not from those of individuality, still having an organ of expression of itself.[1] It is this conviction that constitutes the faith of a Christian in the Resurrection. That faith does not require belief in any particular conception as to the mode of the Resurrection, but the belief that the very person who 'died' on the Cross manifested Himself alive after His death to living men and women; that the experience which came to the earliest witnesses in the form of Vision and Voice was effected by His actual and active personality; that He was still living in His perfected manhood, able to guide and help them. Without this belief there can be no doctrine of the Incarnation, no Gospel, no Church.

---

[1] The heightening of the personality which might be expected in such a case (and is perhaps implied as regards all men in St. Paul's phrase 'clothed upon', 2 Cor. v. 4) is scarcely, I think, reflected in the conversations which represent to us the impression produced on the disciples by the experience. But on the other hand it is probable that this experience affected some of the narratives of the earlier period, so that we have no certain criterion of our Lord's consciousness before and after the Resurrection respectively.

The Appearances of the Risen Lord came to an end. The experience lasted long enough to prove what was to be proved, and "nothing shall prove twice what once was proved". The Ascension was the disciples' interpretation of the cessation of the Appearances and the special character of one of them. The words 'Ascent' and 'Session', which most Christians of the past took literally, convey the same religious meaning when, in this connexion, they have become 'mere' metaphors; but we still have to ask what it is that we mean by them when we have abandoned the idea of any corporeal transference or locomotion, or figurative and illusory transaction analogous to bodily 'levitation' of any kind. We may pause for a moment's thanksgiving that, in no longer being obliged to think of a 'bodily' ascension, we are saved from any need to enter on those hopeless controversies as to the 'locality' of our Lord's Body, which distracted our forefathers and led some of them to evacuate the Sacrament of the Lord's Supper of all its meaning by denying the reality of His 'presence' at it. Indeed, when we think neither of the Resurrection nor of the Ascension as 'bodily' occurrences in any natural or physical sense of the word 'bodily', our thought about the *rationale* of the Sacrament of the Lord's Supper and Sacraments in general is no longer as much bemused as the thought of Christians has been in the past. And the doctrine of the Ascension certainly loses nothing when the fact on which it is based is not supposed to have had a physical expression. The faith we affirm is the faith that our Lord in His perfected manhood passed away from sight to the immediate presence of the Father. We bring our faith into relation to the whole of His human experience in His life on earth. By the words "He ascended into heaven, and sitteth on the right hand of GOD the Father Almighty" we mean to declare our belief in the triumphant issue of the discipline through which He passed (cf. Heb. v. 8) and the completeness of the victory which the world regarded as defeat. And, as we regard Him as the representative of Man, in the victory He won we see the promise of the ascent of redeemed Humanity to GOD and the surety of the fulfilment of the Divine purpose in the creation of Man. To be seated "on the right hand of GOD" means to have attained to the highest place in the sphere of the things of the spirit. The metaphor expresses primarily the idea of honour, the highest recognition of worth. But early teachers were concerned to shew that 'sitting' did not imply inactivity. Kings and judges sit while they exercise their functions of rule and judgement. So, in the faith of a Christian, Christ is King in the spiritual sphere; His will and His ideals rule there, at the very centre of spiritual wisdom and insight and power.

And the Creed goes on : " From thence He shall come to judge the quick and the dead."

These words take us back to the primitive belief in Jesus as Messiah,[1] that He would return to establish on earth the Kingdom of GOD, the reign of righteousness, justice, and truth, and exercise infallible judgement in distinguishing between those who were worthy and those who were unworthy to have place in the regenerate Society. The early Christians lived in the strength of this belief. And though the belief in the ultimate establishment of the Kingdom of GOD on earth, in visible unmistakable reality, gave way either to the idea that the Church itself was the Kingdom, or else to the idea that the Kingdom could only be realized in another life not on earth but in heaven ; this clause remains in the Creed to witness to the Christian conviction that the order of the world as it is does not represent the will of GOD, and that, whether soon or late, as we reckon time, a new order shall be established which will involve a Divine judgement on all that has been and on all who have had part in it.

It does not matter how we conceive of the way

---

[1] See *supra* pp. 50 *ff.*

in which the new order will be established and the judgement effected. We certainly need not be tied to the form of early and persistent beliefs in a 'personal' return of Christ in 'glory' and a universal Judgement Day, when all the nations of the world and all the individual human beings that are still living and have ever lived on earth are gathered together for personal and individual sentences, and punishment or reward. We may regard all these beliefs as to-day we regard the wonderful and often appalling pictures of the great mediaeval artists, which were inspired by them at a time when they formed a very real part of the faith of a Christian. We may even follow up the paths which the Fourth Gospel [1] opens out to us. We may conceive of the 'Second Advent' as a process which has been in progress from the moment of the first experience of the coming of the Spirit; and we may conceive of the 'Judgement' as present and automatic, instant and hourly, not an account a man can postpone to some 'Last Day', but one which he is furnishing for or against himself day by day, as purpose and motive and thought and act write on his character their record.

Yet we cannot in our use of the Creed ignore the

[1] And also St. Luke in his references to the things which Jesus 'began' both to do and to teach (Acts i. 1), which he seems to conceive as still being 'done' by Jesus through His Spirit which came to His Church and might be called either the Spirit of Jesus or the Holy Spirit.

ethical bearings of either of the two beliefs that were associated with the coming again of Christ. Though it is only His function as Judge that is named, and the clause suggests fear rather than hope, the Second Advent has always implied the realization of the Kingdom, and the full faith of a Christian at least includes the hope of a new social organization and order in the world itself; while the religious profession of belief in a Judgement implies the sense of responsibility on the individual's part for the share he has had in making or upholding the organization and the order that is implicitly condemned, and his own acceptance of the principle that the Christianization of actual life in the world, social as well as individual, is possible on a scale that others might think impossible.

We must go a little further and ask ourselves what is implied as to the nature or quality of the Judgement when we say that Christ Himself will be the Judge.

If we retain the personal conception it means that the Judge is one who has the highest possible ideals for men: "Ye shall be perfect, even as your Father is perfect." He is one, too, who conceived of all powers and endowments and attainments as the means and opportunity of social service, who denounced self-seeking in every form and declared willingness to renounce all personal gain and to sacrifice life itself the condition of attaining to the fulness of personality—the full scope of an individual's potential energy and vitality. If a man has the will to keep his life safe, he shall lose it; if he has the will to let it go, he shall save it alive or bring it to a new life. Moreover, the Judge is one who can be terrible in sternness, at least towards every kind of self-satisfaction or religious complacence or intellectual arrogance, and the hardness of the rich and powerful to the poor and weak; and indeed towards every form of disregard of others' needs.

Yet, on the other hand, the judge is Man: one who has lived our life and experienced its difficulties and temptations, and is able to enter fully into the struggle and conflict between the spirit and the flesh. There is mercy, compassion, equity, with Him. Full allowance will be made for ignorance and weakness: all the 'extenuating circumstances' will be borne in mind. Invincible love will contribute its special quality to the righteous judgement. " Mercy glorieth against judgement."

If we drop the personal figure, then, according to the religious construction of this clause of our Creed, we can mean by it no less than to declare our belief that the ideals and standards and values which Jesus upheld, and exhibited in His teaching and life in the world, are the measures by which our own character is to be estimated, and our own personality and life to be weighed. We confess our responsibility and we accept judgement against ourselves in proportion as our achievement falls below "the measure of the stature of the fulness of Christ".

VII

"I BELIEVE IN GOD THE FATHER ALMIGHTY, MAKER OF HEAVEN AND EARTH"

WE return now to the first clauses of the Creed, which, as we have seen, as regards the faith of a Christian are out of the order of experience, and so historically misplaced. It is only on the evidence of the life and experience of Jesus, and in virtue of the valuation of His personality expressed in the central part of the Creed, that we declare our faith in the existence of a GOD whose essential characteristic is represented by the name Father. Before the description "Maker of heaven and earth" was added to the Creed, converts to Christianity from other religions may have associated with the title 'Father' some of the ideas about the relation of GOD to the universe which the same title applied to Him in other religions had implied. We know that Christian apologists of the second and third centuries were prompt to use these ideas as a bridge by which to lead men over to the Christian faith. But the inference that the original intention of the title in the Creed was to express this cosmic relation is surely strangely perverse. It cannot ever have been the primary intention of it. The Christian consciousness of GOD must have been dominated from the first by the conviction that Jesus for the first time in the history of the world had shewn what GOD was really like. Just as many had believed in the coming of the Messiah, but Christians believed that they alone knew who He was—so belief in some kind of GOD was widespread; but Christians, with their conviction that the only true GOD had sent His only Son into the world as man to serve and die for men, were in a position that no others could claim to know exactly the kind of being GOD really was. They alone, by reason of this conviction, had the certainty that the essential characteristic of GOD was love; and they expressed this certainty by the title 'Father' in the Creed. It is this conviction that we affirm, with the inference that follows from it.

Christians inherited from the Jews the belief that the universe was the work of GOD—a belief with which converts from Greek or Roman religion could have no quarrel. But they only put the belief into their Creed when it was called in question within the Christian society itself. The theory of

Creation accepted by the Church, and woven into the fabric of its system, was inevitably based on the narratives of Genesis, regarded as a true account of the way in which the world came into being. We have outgrown this theory, slowly and painfully. Our fathers found it difficult to recognize GOD in 'evolution'. We have learnt to see in it only the description of the way in which, as a matter of fact, He works in Nature; and in learning this, though there are still other things it has to teach us, we have got rid of the old bugbear of Dualism. But it was not to assert any particular conviction as to the way in which Creation was effected that the clause was inserted in the Creed. Its real purpose was not scientific, but religious. It affirms, no doubt, the religious view of the world and the spiritual and moral values of life set out in the story in Genesis. But its primary purpose was to deny and to preclude a positive theory of the Universe which had very strong 'religious' support—the theory that matter, and therefore the whole of man's environment in the world, is either inherently evil and incapable of serving any good and useful purposes (the work of an evil spirit), or else at once unreal and an insidious delusion. This valuation of the universe is the root of the ascetic theory of life, to which reference has already been made. It was the root of the most dangerous theory of the Person of our

VII MAKER OF HEAVEN AND EARTH

Lord which Christians ever conceived — a theory entirely out of relation to the history of His life, making all His experiences as Man an illusion : one which, though formally repudiated by the Church, has profoundly influenced later 'Christian' thought and still haunts some of our doctrines. It is this theory, that the material universe is either evil or unreal, that the clause "Maker of heaven and earth" repels ; and in repelling it and rejecting all dualistic conceptions, and attributing the spiritual and the material alike [1] to the One GOD who is both Father and Almighty, the Creed declares that the world and all that is in it (with all its resources and possibilities) exists for good, that there is a meaning and a purpose in it, and that the meaning and the purpose are good. So by this clause we affirm our faith not only that the world is the outcome and the expression of both power and love, but also that it is under a moral rule. It "means intensely and means good". But the title 'Almighty' needs further comment.

The Greek word which was used in the Greck-speaking parts of the Church ($\pi\alpha\nu\tau o\kappa\rho\acute{\alpha}\tau\omega\rho$) is not well represented by our rendering 'Almighty'. It signifies the exercise of authority or rule, 'all-ruling' or 'ruler of all things', not only having but actively

[1] The addition in Eastern Creeds (*e.g.* our 'Nicene' Creed) of the clause "and of all things visible and invisible" expresses the meaning more fully. Body and soul alike are of His creation.

exercising the power of government in the world. For 'all-mighty', in the sense of simply possessing all power, apart from the idea of its use, there is another word in Greek ($\pi\alpha\nu\tau o\delta\acute{u}\nu\alpha\mu o\varsigma$). Neither of the Greek words seems to have been in common literary use, though both are found in the Greek version of the Old Testament, which was the early Christians' Bible, and the former also a few times in the New Testament.[1] The regular Latin translation of the word used in the Creeds was the equivalent of our 'omnipotent'—a word which bears both senses, 'able to do everything' and 'having power *or* rule over everything'.[2]

It is, of course, much easier to think of GOD as having all power than as actually exercising all power in the world we know. "All things are possible to GOD" Jesus, our Lord, is reported to have said ; and, though it was with a curiously limited immediate reference that He used the words, the conviction that there is nothing GOD cannot do is elementary in the religious consciousness of men. The belief that there is no limit to His power is the

[1] Only, however, in a quotation of LXX, Amos iv. 13, in 2 Cor. vi. 18, and nine times in the Apocalypse. Cf. the word 'autocrat', sole-ruler ($\alpha\dot{u}\tau o\kappa\rho\acute{a}\tau\omega\rho$), as a title of the Roman Emperor, found even as early as coins of Julius Caesar, and $\kappa o\sigma\mu o\kappa\rho\acute{a}\tau o\rho\epsilon\varsigma$, Eph. vi. 12, of the devils or 'princes of the air', which Hilary translated *mundipotentes*, 'rulers of the world'.

[2] *Omnipotens*. Tertullian, however, and Augustine rendered it by *omnitenens*, and others (*e.g.* Prudentius) by *omnipollens*, both being words which convey the idea of the active exercise of power.

basis of nearly all petitionary prayer, and the stay of the believer in his utmost straits. No disciple of Jesus could have put any limit to the power of GOD. But to the exercise of that power every Christian knows that there are limitations.

No Christian supposes that his GOD, who is essentially holy and loving, could ever exercise His power except for ends of righteousness and love—the ends which He wills. The moral nature, as we call it, of GOD—as Christians conceive Him—is thus a very real limitation of His power; and when in the Creed we profess our belief in Him as 'almighty', we are declaring our faith in a GOD for whom it is impossible to will, and therefore impossible to do, anything inconsistent with the highest ideals of the Fatherhood which we attribute to Him in all His relations with us.

We are obliged to use the word 'limitation'; but the fact that we have to use such a word in such a connexion is a symptom of our own limitations, not only of the poverty of our language, but of our moral conceptions themselves. For, as Augustine taught us long ago, the *beata necessitas non peccandi*, not only the happy impossibility of sinning, but the Divine constraint always to do right, is the note of real moral freedom. To be unable to will or to do anything that does not subserve the highest moral ends, to be limited in the use of powers always to

L

the one line of direction that is in all conceivable circumstances the right line, to have such a personality or being or nature or character that it can never find expression except in righteousness and love : this is really to be free from limitation, to be independent, to exercise full sovereignty and lordship over everything that exists and in everything that happens. It is in this sense that the 'Almighty' GOD of our Christian Creed is limited; for the energy, the activity, of His rule in the world can never deviate from the path that leads to the full attainment of His ends. And as we believe Him to be Almighty in this sense, we are also, by using the word, avowing our faith that the good purpose which we believe is being worked out through all the pain and passion of life as we know it will be achieved. We range ourselves with the optimists —not those who make light of the evil, whose attitude is indicated in Pope's lines :

> Whatever wrong we call
> May, must be, right as relative to all—

but the higher optimists who know the fierce reality of the evil and yet believe in the ultimate triumph of the good.

But there is another 'limitation' of His power. When we think of GOD as ruler of the world, whether 'present' in it or actively controlling its destiny from 'outside' it, we have to take account of all the evil, mental, moral, and physical, that exists in the world—of all the pain and suffering and all the apparent waste and failure of life. When we avow our faith in "GOD the Father Almighty", do we mean that these things are willed by Him? and if not, does not their existence prohibit the use of the word 'almighty' of Him in any natural sense? The question is put in the form of a dilemma: GOD is either not all-loving, or not all-ruling; either power or love may be predicated of Him, but not both.

Christians have commonly refused to accept this dilemma, and the two words side by side in the Creed register their refusal. They have also given the right reason, though they have made very sparing use of it in any other connexion than this. It was GOD's will to create the world and human beings in His image, beings with power of self-determination, not automatons or puppets: and by willing the existence of other intelligences, capable of resisting His will and purpose for them, He willed the limitation of His own control over them so far as was needed for the end to which He destined them. He only controls them so far as He can do so while leaving them free agents, to be trained by the use of powers and affections which He has given them, to become free personalities after His own likeness.

We remind ourselves again that it is only the poverty of our language and our conceptions that obliges us to speak of this method as involving a limitation of the power of GOD. Could we judge the whole course of human history as absolute power and love would judge it, could we read the chronicle of human souls as GOD would read it, we should be in a position to criticize the method. Meanwhile our experience of the best results that are visible to us of the method is sufficient to allow the faith that He is 'Almighty' and that the evil in the world, intensely real as it is, is only contingent on the working out and ultimate realization of His purpose as 'Father'.

But when we have allowed their full scope to these two 'limitations', there remains another consideration of the highest importance in determining the religious construction of this clause of the Creed. In the Lord's Prayer we have the petition "Thy kingdom come, Thy will be done, on earth as in heaven"—a petition which means that the rule of GOD is not effectively established on earth, nor His will in full operation.

As He cannot will anything but the fruits of righteousness and love, so He does not will these things in the world except as the spontaneous response of human wills and affections. All our Lord's teaching on prayer and His own practice in His life on earth imply the need of man's co-operation with GOD for the realization of His ends. The very Incarnation itself, as we have seen, implies that it is only through man that GOD can work effectively in the world. Men are His agents, and unless they fulfil their office right, His rule, by His own will, is not effective. He will not force those over whom He rules. There is no conscription: they must volunteer for His service: it is a great adventure to which He calls them. And there is no immunity from pain and suffering guaranteed to those who respond. Pleasure is not offered—the word had been too much profaned; but peace and happiness, surpassing the peace and happiness of ordinary experience in a world which reflects so much of the beauty and love of the Father who made it, and even joy, are to be the concomitants and the 'reward' of faithful service. In the way of achievement on these lines the 'impossible' does not exist for the Christian.

This is to say that GOD has given the world a constitution and governs it according to that constitution. It is a rule that allows all kinds of 'natural' disasters and physical and moral suffering, till men learn the constitution and obey it. It is not religious to ask that GOD will suspend that constitution, when the business of life is to find out its purpose and its secrets and live according to them. This kind of rule allowed Jesus to be crucified. It allows many forms of insensate cruelty and injustice, conscious and unconscious, to this day. Yet life under a Ruler of this kind is surely life worth living, and the personality that may be created and developed by such a method, in conscious co-operation with such a sovereignty, is a personality that a rule more absolute could never produce.

So by this phrase of the Creed we turn our back on all suggestions of a GOD who is really limited in power, or one who hardly knows what He wants—an immanent will of the universe struggling to come to consciousness of Itself, its purpose as well as Itself being still 'in the making'. We affirm our faith in a Will both wise and benevolent, a Purpose clearly defined, and a Power infallibly and unswervingly directed to the best means of achieving its ends. And this Divine personality, His will, His purpose, and the means to its fulfilment, we see revealed in Jesus Christ, His only Son, our Lord.

Christians have even sometimes gone so far as to suppose that the very purpose of the Incarnation, the assumption of manhood by the Son of GOD, was to make the Crucifixion possible. The Christian conception of the character of GOD is at any rate entirely dominated by the belief that the crucified

Jesus was His Son, very GOD of very GOD; and in the Resurrection and Ascension of the Crucified the Christian sees the transfiguration of the Cross and the vindication of the method of GOD'S rule in the world.

VIII

"I BELIEVE IN THE HOLY GHOST; THE HOLY CATHOLIC CHURCH; THE COMMUNION OF SAINTS; THE FORGIVENESS OF SINS; THE RESURRECTION OF THE BODY, AND THE LIFE EVERLASTING"

IN our study of the Apostles' Creed, so far, we have seen that the conception of GOD which it sets before us is one that depends on the specific valuation of our Lord's personality and life, which it is the object of the Creed to affirm. But the Creed goes on to complete the doctrine of GOD, by declaring belief in the Holy Ghost—co-ordinated with the Father and the Son.

The doctrine of the Holy Spirit, the Spirit of the Father and of the Son, is like all other doctrines an interpretation, a rationalization, of experience. How far it was conditioned by our Lord's actual teaching to His disciples cannot be determined with any certainty: the whole problem of the authorship, sources, historical exactitude, and literary method of the Fourth Gospel is involved in an answer to that question. But that our Lord had spoken of the Spirit, and had bidden His disciples look to an influx of the Spirit to guide and strengthen them, must I think be regarded as certain. The Fourth Gospel represents a definite gift of the Holy Spirit by our Lord Himself on the evening of the day of the Resurrection (Jn. xx. 22 f.); St. Luke, on the other hand, represents the promise of the gift, which will be a gift from the Father, as renewed in our Lord's last words before the Ascension, and the consciousness of possession of it as realized first on the day of Pentecost (Acts i. 4, 8; ii.).

Both accounts agree in their witness to a definite spiritual experience which the disciples had, an experience which they believed to be caused by the Spirit of Jesus or of His Father, assuring them of the continuance of their relation with Him. The same experience was renewed again and again, and the belief in the existence of the Holy Spirit became as well established as the belief in the Father and the Son, as an interpretation of actual religious experience. Of this fact there can be no doubt, whether its origination is to be traced back to suggestion on our Lord's part or not.

We cannot now enter on any details of the history of the definition of the doctrine as we find it expressed in other Creeds than the Apostles' and in other formularies of the Church. The process was a slow one. There was no doubt about the reality of the experience; but was the Spirit to which it was attributed to be regarded as a manifestation of the personality of the living and glorified Jesus, or was it a Divine energy to be distinguished in some way from His Spirit? Or again, was it hardly to be centralized in GOD at all? The definition of the experience, as of all other religious experience, was a purely intellectual problem, and the *intelligentsia* of the Church were long in coming to agreement. The only part of the definition that has special interest for us is one that is of late date in formal statements of belief, and, when it made its way into the Latin version of the Nicene Creed, became a chief cause of disagreement and disunion between the Church of the East and the Church of the West. It is the part that defines faith in the Holy Spirit as faith in One " who proceedeth from the Father and the Son ". In this definition it is only the addition of the words 'and the Son' that concerns us. They are entirely in harmony with early Christian sentiment and conviction. Without the Son nothing would have been known of the Spirit, and the connexion between the Spirit and Jesus in the minds of His disciples was vital. The evidence of the Fourth Gospel is conclusive on a point like this. It is only through Jesus that it will come to them: in their experience at least He will be the originator of the new sense, the new power. He Himself had lived His life in the world in the power of the Spirit of GOD—this is the fact about Him on which the earliest preaching laid its stress, and the assurance of this Divine influence which He Himself had was one of the facts of life of which His disciples must take account; when they too had a similar experience, it came to them mediated through Him. And the addition of the words 'and the Son' emphasizes the fact that the doctrine of the Holy Spirit rests upon the same historical basis as the doctrine of the Person of Christ, and is in the same way an interpretation of actual facts of human experience. The Creed, as we have seen, is Christo-centric. In interpreting Jesus Christ, Christians came to know GOD under three aspects, as Father, as Son, and as Holy Spirit. And when they reasoned out their experience they framed the doctrine of the Trinity: one GOD existing eternally in three modes of being, three relationships. The Latin-speaking Christians expressed these relations within the Being of GOD by the word *persona* (person), which in its theological use retained its early meaning of status or condition or character of existence. The idea of three 'persons' in the popular sense of the English word is carefully excluded in the Athanasian Creed by its repeated refrain 'not three . . . but one . . .', yet only at the price—to ordinary ears—of making nonsense of the Creed and encouraging the popular idea that Theology is learned mystification. The Apostles' Creed by itself does not exclude tritheistic conceptions at all.

In the 'Nicene' Creed, in like manner, though tritheism is formally denied by the statement of belief in 'one GOD' and by the definitions of the 'one Lord Jesus Christ' and 'the Holy Ghost the Lord and Giver of Life', there are no obvious safeguards against the conception of a graduated Godhead; and, indeed, that conception was in favour, as a solution of some theological puzzles, with some of the most honoured theologians of the fourth century. It is reflected in the 'Nicene' Creed itself in the phrase 'one GOD the Father', a collocation of words which suggests the idea that 'the Father' is GOD in a sense in which the others are not GOD. To make the Father the 'fountain of Godhead', from which the Godhead of the Son and the Spirit is derived, or to bring into the Godhead the idea of one cause and two effects, is to press the analogy of human experience too far; even if we apply to it what Augustine said of the use of the word 'person', that we only use it to save ourselves from being reduced to saying nothing. We are far enough to-day from being able to put into words what 'personality' is: but at least we know something of what it consists in. It is for us, what it was not when Christian doctrines were defined, a real instrument of thought. It is the 'personality' of GOD that concerns us. If we know that, we know Him. The philosophy of the universe may require the Absolute: Religion demands a Person. And however the personality of GOD may transcend our thought, there must be in Him that which corresponds to personality in us. He cannot be less a Person than we are persons. What the doctrine of the Trinity affirms of the personality of GOD is represented by the three relationships of Father, Son, and Spirit. No one of these alone is GOD. In the Christian conception of GOD, Father, Son, and Spirit are alike and equally essential to His Being. There never was One of the Three alone: the Three together are GOD. The essence of 'His personality is thought of as consisting in relationships—the capacity for communion and the active exercise of that communion.[1] The GOD of the faith of a Christian contains within Himself the

---

[1] The doctrine of the eternal generation of the Son, as a continuous process 'outside' Time (very inadequately expressed in the words of the Nicene Creed 'begotten of the Father before all ages'), and again the clause of the Nicene Creed that describes the Son ('very GOD of very GOD', 'consubstantial with the Father') as the medium 'through whom all things were created', represent this continuous output of energy and constant expression of itself in action and reaction as essential factors in the personality of GOD.

'social' sense in full activity. He is the actual energy of social life, eternally expressing and realizing Himself in love and its attendant sacrifice. It was our Lord's own experience on earth that taught Him to say, If a man will save his life, he shall lose it, and if he will lose it, he shall save it alive; but in laying down this cardinal principle of Christian ethics, He did not only proclaim the way by which human personality in its fulness is created, He revealed the essential nature of the personality of GOD.

So in affirming in the Apostles' Creed our belief in the Holy Ghost we complete the definition of the GOD in whom we profess our faith. But we also do something more.

The Holy Spirit represents to us not only an eternal factor of the personality of GOD, but also His action on the world and us. It is indeed the idea of GOD 'in action' in the world, in the minds and wills and hearts of men, from the beginning of the world's existence and more particularly, generation after generation, in the Church, that the clause in the Creed is intended to affirm. It was to their actual experience of the working of the Spirit in them that St. Paul turned his rather unstable converts for evidence of the truth of the Gospel he preached, and the belief that the Spirit of GOD is really operative in the Christian Society has always been the fundamental bond of fellowship among Christians. "It seemed good to the Holy Ghost and to us." This conviction has no doubt been present at times when the Church has erred in its judgements both as to faith and as to morals. No claim to infallibility can be established, if infallibility be given its popular meaning, implying a decision which is fixed for ever and of permanent force and validity. But if, on the other hand, a more modest claim be made, the case is different. If Christians are constantly conscious of the working in them of a power which is not 'their own', which guides them to good; and if the Church, when it had to choose between alternatives and make collective decisions, generally chose the alternative which made for truth and righteousness and kept the way open for future progress; then we have as much evidence as we can want to justify belief in the guidance of the Holy Spirit. We expect too much if we suppose that, because a decision was reached which was right in the particular complex of conditions, it must be an ultimate and final expression of truth in all circumstances. To suppose this is to ignore the refraction of the human medium through which the Divine illumination must pass, and to act as if the process of the world stood still. It is to ignore all that we know of the method of GOD'S working by experimental stages in His continuous and progressive education of mankind.

The presence of the Holy Spirit in the Church does not guarantee to any particular generation the insight into the circumstances of a later age which is needed if final decisions are to be reached; and it is not Religion but Conservatism that is the parent of the theory that such decisions are irreformable. If this very simple truth could be more widely recognized we might be content to differ in amity as to the exact measure of authority which ought to be attached to precedent. A belief or a formula or an institution that is already in possession has the prestige which lawfully belongs to the best our ancestors could devise or do. It is not presumptuous in a later generation to believe that the guidance of the Holy Spirit which their ancestors enjoyed is quite as fully at their own disposal. It is in the present quite as much as in the past activity of the Spirit, in the world in general and in the Church and individual Christians, that we declare our faith.

The articles of the Creed that follow the clause on the Holy Spirit are all dependent on this belief and organically connected with it. It is this doctrine of the Holy Spirit that controls the meaning of the clauses on the Church and the Communion of Saints; the forgiveness of sins; the resurrection of the body and everlasting life. They all express manifestations of the working, the operations, of the

Spirit, and declare the belief that the same Divine power which is the source of the true life of all men, which was uniquely operative in Jesus Christ, is also operative in Christians as members of the Society of Jesus—the more effectively in proportion to the sensitiveness of their consciousness as Christians. Individuals may win a real spiritual union with God, real fellowship with the faithful of all times, forgiveness of sins, the resurrection from the dead which is eternal life. But it is not the individualistic conception of the attainment of these spiritual good things that the Creed expresses. It is the social conception.[1] The individual is not isolated, does not stand alone, is not thought of in the Christian Creed as separate from his fellows. The very existence of the Christian Society is the chief monument of the Spirit's work.

Extra ecclesiam nulla salus is an aphorism that may be applied in narrow and misleading ways, but it certainly expresses the essential meaning of these clauses of the Apostles' Creed. Life is organic, and there is a science of its organization. The perfection of human personality is only to be attained by the careful ordering of each human life in relation to each other. This perfection of human personality

[1] The conception is emphasized in an African form of the Apostles' Creed, which gives the last section as follows: "We believe also in the Holy Spirit, the forgiveness of sins, the resurrection of the flesh, and eternal life *through the Holy Church.*"

—the salvation which is of faith in Jesus Christ—is to be won within One Holy Catholic Church. This primitive conviction has never altogether faded from the consciousness of Christians. In the past, when divisions arose within the Church and schisms took place, the seceding body of Christians always claimed to represent the one true Church, and to be upholding the true standard of holiness and Catholic teaching; and it was always willing to enrol as members all other Christians—who agreed with it. "*We* are the true Church", and salvation is to be obtained by membership of our Church :—this has been in the past the conviction of every organized body of Christians.

There is, of course, no doubt as to the historical meaning of the belief expressed in the Apostles' and the Nicene Creeds. The Church is the Society, or the Societies, that can shew unbroken continuity with the Church of the Apostles, in faith, in ministry, and in sacraments. In the world it is localized here and there, but everywhere it represents and is *the* Catholic Church. Through this Church the gifts of the Holy Spirit, forgiveness, resurrection, eternal life, are mediated.

And if a wider interpretation is justified in the light of experience, none at least is possible which does not recognize at once the 'supernatural' and the social character of Christian life. It is through the Holy Spirit—the spirit of Jesus, the spirit of GOD—and in active co-operation with the organized life, the worship and sacraments, of the Christian Society that individuals realize themselves, become the best they are capable of becoming, win in a word 'salvation'. It is an old accepted principle in the Church that GOD is not limited by His sacraments. What we express in the Creed is the belief that He does work through all the institutions of the Church, and that through membership in the organic body of a Society definitely Christian in its outlook and ideals the guidance and gifts of His Holy Spirit are to be won.

The Christian theory of life is social. It is expressed by the phrase 'the Kingdom of God': it is membership of a divinely ordered *Society* that our Lord's teaching had always in view as the goal for men to aim at; and the qualifications which he inculcated could only be realized in a society. All the specific Christian virtues are social virtues. Christian personality is a creation of social life. To attain the Kingdom of GOD men must be drawn into active co-operation with their fellows; they must realize the law of the Kingdom in such intimate relationship as exists between the members of a body and the body as a whole. The Church is at once a Society of Saints, in idea and partly in realization, *and* a School of Saints; and in the Creed it is in the Society primarily, and only in individuals as members of it, that the Holy Spirit is conceived as operative.

A Christian's belief in the Church is thus the concentrated expression of his belief in the dependence of human society on GOD. But, if ever there could be established in the world a society organized on the principles of Christian Ethics, and permeated with the spirit of the life and teaching of Jesus, there would be a Church such as the historical Catholic Church has never yet been, if it has even ever consistently tried to be. The fellowship of Christians one with another, the Communion of Saints, the Unity of the Spirit in the bond of love, has not yet been realized within the Church itself. We declare our belief that it can be, and we affirm the ideal as our own.

It has been suggested that the phrase 'the Communion of Saints' (*sanctorum communionem*) represents an original Greek ἁγίων κοινωνία and meant 'participation in the holy things', that is, 'in the Sacraments'—κοινωνία having a concrete sense and referring to outward and visible fellowship.[1] So the clause would emphasize the benefits of

---

[1] Cf. the deacon's proclamation τὰ ἅγια τοῖς ἁγίοις (*sancta sanctis*) before the consecration in some ancient liturgies.

VIII THE COMMUNION OF SAINTS

the Sacraments as a chief result of membership of the Church, and the phrase *communionem sacramentorum* which Augustine uses would be its equivalent.

But Augustine also uses the expressions *communio sanctorum* and *societas sanctorum* (masculine, not neuter) to express the fellowship which members of the Church have with one another, from which heretics are excluded.[1] In this usage the phrase may be almost equivalent to the congregation or church of the Saints as a visible unit; but the wider conception of fellowship with all the faithful of all times is not excluded. The belief in this fellowship is inherent in St. Paul's conception of the members of the one Body, and in the Johannine allegory of the Vine and the branches; and it can never have been absent from the consciousness of the Church. And when the clause first appears in the Creed of Niceta of Remesiana, he explains it in this widest sense. These are his words: "What is the Church but the congregation of all saints? For from the beginning of the world, be they patriarchs . . . or prophets or apostles or martyrs or all other righteous men, who have been, who are, who will be, all are one Church, because hallowed by one faith and manner of life, sealed by one Spirit, they are made one body:

[1] *Serm.* 52, 117, and cf. *c. Faustum* xvi. 16.

and of this Body the Head is . . . Christ. . . .
Therefore in this one Church thou believest that
thou wilt attain to the *communion of saints.*"[1] And
though at a later date stress is occasionally laid
on the idea of communion in holy things, and
fellowship in the sacraments has always been a
mark of membership in the Church, it is belief in
the intimate union and conjunction of all believers
with one another in Christ—a union not broken
by death—which the clause has commonly been
understood to express. And so it interprets the
meaning of the Church and membership of it as
passing beyond the limits of time and space.

As members of the historical Church of Christ
we are heirs of a tradition amazingly rich in its
record of spiritual endeavour and achievement;
and if we consciously take up our inheritance in
this Great Church, it is much more than a tradition
that is ours. We do not only catch the accents
of the religious heroes of the past and learn a
great creative language, by which our own thoughts
and ideals are moulded. Nor are we only linked
with them in a community of aim and aspiration
and hope and faith, expressed in worship and
sacramental rites. We actually share their life.
The stream of creative energy which flowed from
the spirit of GOD through them, and still sustains

[1] *De symbolo* 10.

them, becomes for us too, through them, the energy by which we in turn are recreated and live the life of faith.

We have professed our belief in 'the Communion of Saints', but that Communion of Saints can only be if there has first been forgiveness of sins; for to the religious consciousness, facing the facts of experience, the communion of sinners is the more present and insistent reality. The forgiveness of sins, or its equivalent, it has been the aim of all Religions to attain. It is the Christian's conception of GOD and man's relation to Him that gives a special character to the forgiveness of sins in which we profess our belief. Only in this sense is it true to describe 'forgiveness' as 'Christ's greatest innovation in ethics', and the description is not true at all so far as it suggests the idea that forgiveness is purely ethical. It is the whole personality that is at stake, and sin, according to the truly Christian conception of it, is something— anything—that mars personality and prevents or impedes its developement in life to the end for which, in Creation, GOD destined it. So the sinner is always a sinner 'against himself'. Whether in thought, or in feeling, or in action—or by the lack of thought and feeling and action when need of it is present—so far as in him lies, he is arresting the fulfilment of the design of GOD as regards himself and all his fellow-creatures. A Christian man's whole religious duty is to realize as vividly as he can the purpose of GOD and to co-operate with Him, as fully and as consciously as he can. It is one of the strangest paradoxes in the history of Christianity that the words 'religious duties' should have the sense they usually bear, and that the observance of rites and ceremonies, and days and seasons, and the acceptance of formulas, all of which are of man's making as means to the end, should be regarded as the criterion of a man's status before GOD.[1] The Church has been slow to understand that when Jesus denounced the ecclesiasticism of the religious leaders of His time, He denounced the ecclesiasticism of all religions and all times, and many of the 'sins' which have loomed large in her eyes in the past have been offences against her own ecclesiastical system. In her practice in this respect the motive of the Church may have been ethical—the maintenance of an order of life is part of the business of any Society which exists for ethical ends. But this manufacture by the Church of 'ecclesiastical' sins is one, at least, of the reasons why a thinker of the highest character can tell us that the last thing a healthy-

[1] I have referred in the Preface (p. xx. note) to a recent statement which reflects this perverted view.

minded man troubles himself about to-day is his 'sins'. Often, too, in the past, as Dr. Tennant[1] has reminded us, there has been confusion between offences and shortcomings that are ethical in character and those that are really only 'aesthetic'. A 'profane oath', for example, may be no more really 'profane' than expressions common in 'polite society'; indeed, it often only reveals the limited range of the speaker's vocabulary, and is not even an 'aesthetic' sin. It is not of 'sins' such as these that we need to think in connexion with this clause of the Creed.

Nor, again, by using it, are we declaring belief in the efficacy of the means provided by the ecclesiastical system for procuring forgiveness, in the sense that no other means are efficacious. The phrase itself, in collocation with the Church, does, however, clearly imply the social character of sin and the responsibility of the whole Society for the character and lives of its members. It is as members of a Society that we make our profession, and if, in the mind of the Church, the sins in view are offences of the individual against GOD, they are also offences against the Society, from which the Society must seek to guard itself, even though they arise from its own neglect of its collective duty to its members. Their effects pass over from the member to the body

[1] See F. H. Tennant *The Concept of Sin.*

and hinder it from functioning aright. The personality of the whole Society is injuriously affected; and the Society, acting through its appointed representatives, has a right to determine the conditions on which it gives its corporate absolution. They are not necessarily conditions on which GOD gives His.

We declare our belief that of all such sins there is 'forgiveness'; and the word means, in its Greek and Latin equivalents, absolute putting away, and implies the reinstatement of the sinner, or his establishment in a status free from sin, in which the consequences of his sin on others are not reckoned against him. It was one of the charges levelled against Christians in early days that they welcomed sinners to their fold and treated their sins as null and void. But the Christian apologist replied to the effect that, though it was impossible to undo a thing once done, or catch up and arrest its results, the essence of sin lay not in the thing done, but in the will of him who did it, and when once the person's will was changed from evil to good the sin was blotted out. The early discipline of the Church and its penitential system was directed to the end of securing that such a change of will should really take place or had already been accomplished. To inflict 'punishment' is not the business of a religious Society: that must be left to GOD, and perhaps to States. The only kind of discipline which is consistent with Christian ideals is remedial and reformative, and a Christian or a Christian Society that has any other motive in the exercise of power than the best developement of personality fails to act up to its ideal. It is the personal aspect and the personal results of sin with which alone it is concerned, and in declaring our belief in the forgiveness of sins we affirm our faith in the illimitable possibility of a new direction being given to the will and a new start being made towards the perfection of the personality.

Our Lord seems to have spoken of the possibility of sin so destructive and deadly as to preclude the chance of renewal, and St. John's recognition of 'sin unto death' may be an echo of His words. We cannot determine exactly what form of sin our Lord had in mind—the sin 'against the Holy Spirit' may well be different in different persons and at different times. From the context He seems to have meant at the moment a sin against light, a wilful refusal to face the facts, and the attribution of evil motives and sinister designs to a rival whose works were conspicuously good. There certainly is no reason to suppose that the 'deadly sins' of the Church's classification would have been regarded by Him as sins which can have no forgiveness either here or hereafter.

In the Creed at any rate we make no distinction, and we do not pledge ourselves to any of the distinctions the Church has made in the past. We set no limits to our faith in the restorative and re-creative power of Mercy and Love—the Mercy and Love which is also Righteousness

> nor spares skin surface
> Smoothening Truth away.

Our Creed concludes with the profession of belief in "the Resurrection of the body and the life everlasting". The latter part of this statement is the more general expression of the faith which the whole is intended to declare, but it was a comparatively late addition that had no place in the Western Creed at the end of the fourth century; and it is the clause "the Resurrection of the body" that chiefly claims attention. We of the reformed Church of England were the first among Christians to express our faith in these terms in a Creed. The phrase 'of the flesh' is the oldest form in Creeds, still retained in the order of the Church of Rome and by ourselves in the Creed in use in Baptism. The resurrection 'of the flesh' expressed the actual belief of nearly all Christians till recent times. One well-known Church in the fourth century had a Creed in use that emphasized the general belief by inserting the word 'this' before 'flesh'; and one of the questions regularly put to bishops in the public examination as to their faith which was part of the ceremony of their consecration, throughout, it seems, the Middle Ages, was even more explicit: " Dost thou believe", it ran, " in the resurrection of this flesh which thou now hast on thee?" The more general expression "the resurrection of the dead" was of course in use in the Creed of the Eucharist, but individual teachers who shrank from the phrase 'of the flesh' were always regarded with suspicion. It is commonly said that the phrase has no warrant in the New Testament, and certainly it is impossible to reconcile it with the ideas of the future life that St. Paul sets before us: and he is the chief, almost the only, exponent of a Christian's reasoned faith on the subject in the apostolic age. He bases his faith in the resurrection of men so explicitly on the Resurrection of Jesus, and so clearly regards the 'body' which will be theirs as a distinct creation fitted for a new and distinct environment, that it is hard to believe that he knew, or accepted in its literal sense, the story that our Lord appeared to the disciples in ' flesh and bones'. Yet there, in the Gospel written by his own companion, the story stood for future generations; and in the later Gospel of St. John it assumed a form that captured the imagination of Christians, as it holds it still. So, in the typical example of Resurrection, the one case as to which any details about the manner of it were forthcoming, the 'body' was characterized as having flesh; and Christians, who read this story as a literal statement of the actual facts, naturally assumed that they too, when they entered on the life of the Resurrection, would have flesh. The belief is entirely congruous with the belief that the Risen Lord had a body of flesh and bones. We rest our faith as Christians on His experience as Man; it is His Resurrection that we hope to share; and we have no authority for any opinion about the manner of our own resurrection except such as the analogy of His supplies. The passing away of belief in our own resurrection in the flesh—of belief, that is, in the literal truth of the clause in the Creed which we profess at Baptism, and ratify at Confirmation—is an instance of those changes in our outlook which destroy the unity of the Creed, unless we may interpret the clause "On the third day He rose again from the dead" in a sense analogous to our interpretation of the clause "the resurrection of the body".[1]

---

[1] The *impasse* which the traditional theology and scholarship have reached at the moment is illustrated in the argument of a distinguished scholar and divine for whom I must always feel the highest respect. He justified the two phrases 'of the flesh' and 'of the body' equally with the less definite, and preferable, phrase 'of the dead' on the ground that 'all flesh is not the same flesh' and that 'there are bodies celestial as well as bodies terrestrial'. You may say 'of the flesh' without meaning flesh of any kind known to us, and you may say 'of the body' while meaning a body quite other than that which

In the discussion of that clause according to its religious construction, its significance was seen to lie in the faith that the personality of Jesus, as fashioned by the experience of His whole life in the world, survived His death as man. That He should have powers after death which we cannot have, except in part, would be congruous with our belief that His personality in His human life had a potency which is not ours, except in part. The 'body' here in our experience is the organ of our individual personality, and our faith in the resurrection of the body is our faith in the survival of our personal identity with the capacity for self-expression.

In view of the history of the past and the continuous associations of the clause, we cannot use it as the expression of our faith if all that we mean to affirm is the survival of 'a stream of tendency' or of the effects of our thoughts and actions here on future generations. We cannot use it, that is, if we only mean some kind of 'corporate' immortality in which we shall have no conscious share—the results of our conscious activities simply passing over to the wider life of the race, conceived as somehow enriched by them, and being incorporated in it.

---

we wear in this life. What you must not say is 'of *this* flesh' (*Journal of Theological Studies* vol. xviii. p. 141). Yet it was just in these terms that a bishop in his examination before consecration had to confess his belief. It is surely time to get behind all these phrases to the religious convictions for which they stood.

We cannot use the clause in any such sense as this; for what personality contributes to the progress of humanity is just itself; and if that personality comes to an end, then it is the achievement itself that is lost.

But we can still use the clause in the religious sense it has always borne, although we do not believe that at a last Judgement Day we shall appear at the great Assize in the bodies in which we now are. We can even use the vivid phrase of the ancient creeds, and of our own Church in its most solemn act of admitting new members to its fellowship, and declare our belief in the resurrection 'of the flesh' (or even 'of *this* flesh'), if it is our faith that we ourselves in our human personalities, as we are in the days of the flesh, with all things appertaining to the completeness of man's nature — no bare and empty disembodied 'spirits', but as we have been made by all our life's experience—will live again after death and 'receive' the things done in the body, according to what we have done, whether it be good or bad.

Christian sentiment loves to dwell on the thought of the redemption of the body. But we know that it is the person in it who needs to be redeemed. The body in its normal condition in this life, with all its amazing adaptability and unity in diversity, is already a marvellous organ for the expression of the individual's personality, whether it be good or bad. And unless it is 'redeemed' from the lower uses to which it may be put in this life (and redeemed it must be if the person whose organ it is is redeemed) there is no warrant for supposing that anything that happens in death can redeem it. Whatever the 'body' of the future life may be, it is the Christian belief that it will be the expression of the personality itself. " For soul is form, and doth the body make."

As to what will be the nature of that second life we do not in our Creed declare belief. Many and various, attractive and repellent, have been the ideas that Christians have had of the future life. Hopes and fears have jostled each other. Of none of these do we either give or withhold our acceptance by professing our faith in the terms of the Creed. The veil has scarcely been lifted. Our Lord Himself we are only able to follow, by the historical evidence we have, into the first court, as it were, or the nearest 'mansion', of the life beyond the grave. We infer, by analogy, that the change is at least 'by no loss at all'—no loss of personality; what may be 'the adding'[1] we can do little more than guess. The word 'everlasting' only suggests that the life goes on and on in time; but we are not committed by the phrase, in its historical meaning, to any theory of Time, as to whether it is real or not. For our

[1] James Hinton, *Life and Letters* p. 182.

equivalent of both the Greek and the Latin words is 'eternal', and the Nicene phrase translated 'the life of the world to come' means the 'eternal' life that follows this. It is only relatively to this life that the phrase suggests the idea of succession. By itself it does not even suggest continuity, as the former clause in the Creed undoubtedly does. It rather suggests a break of some kind. We are free in our use of the clause to think, with St. John, of the life eternal as a way of living now—a life on which we enter when we know GOD and Jesus Christ as sent by Him, or when we set our wills to do His will—a life which will be achieved in its fulness hereafter, but a life of which we have no warrant, except our Christian faith in GOD as Father and Creator of all that exists, unless we begin it here.

Or we are free to believe with the Pope, in *The Ring and the Book*, that the sudden 'shock' and 'surprise' of Death may be sufficient to awaken the capacity for eternal life that is latent in every man who is made " in the image of GOD ", and so, that we may

> see, one instant, and be saved.

IX

READJUSTMENT

"THE modern defenders of the Faith, who would put the clock back and reinstate (and, if they could, impose by 'superior authority' on others) all kinds of primitive and mediaeval conceptions, which the world has outgrown, are becoming impossible. But then, so also are the Creeds, if it is only by this kind of interpretation that they can be retained. It was a mistake ever to introduce them into the public Services and Common Prayer of the Church, and they ought to be put away in the archives of the Church among its title-deeds and only inspected now and then by the historians of the Faith. Christianity is really in possession, and if its title is seriously disputed, it will not be established by an appeal to any kind of authority or prescriptive right. It will have to justify itself as it is to-day, not only to the quickened moral conscience of mankind, which it has done so much to mould, but also to the awakening mind or intelligence of the masses, which the Church as a whole has been little concerned to liberate in the past."

These words sum up a widespread opinion, which the writer of the foregoing pages of this book in large measure shares. If 'this kind of interpretation' of the Creeds is impossible, the Creeds themselves have become impossible. Our judgement as to whether 'this kind of interpretation' of the Creeds is possible or not will be determined, I suppose, by our estimate of 'miracle'. With regard to this great subject only one dominant consideration may be mentioned here.[1] No period has been as fruitful as the last twenty or thirty years in study of the beginnings of Christianity, of all the conditions of life and thought, of popular piety and theological and philosophical speculation, in the midst of which the earliest interpretations of the facts of our Lord's life, and of the great stream of religious experience which had its spring in those facts, were fashioned. And one result of this study is that the Christian student is much more sure of the reality of this religious experience, and of the impression produced by our Lord, of His 'impact' on the world, than he

[1] Far and away the best book on the subject is J. Wendland's *Miracles and Christianity* (Eng. trans., Hodder & Stoughton, 1911). Most other books in English are mischievously apologetic, and do not face the real facts and arguments that have to be met. I may be allowed to refer to some pages of my own in *The Hibbert Journal* (vol. xiv. pp. 830-833).

is of the ways in which that impression was produced. The interpretation of it in our Gospels is, he is sure, very largely controlled by preconceptions. Convinced as he may be with regard to the central figure of the whole story that he that hath seen Him hath seen the Father, and that He is the Way, the Truth and the Life, he cannot distinguish nearly so sharply as Christian apologists have distinguished in the past, between the records of 'miracles' in the Gospels and elsewhere. He sees that religious thought of all ages has always expressed its belief in Divine action and activity in terms of the 'miraculous': No miracle, no GOD. And the question presents itself to him whether 'the miraculous' is not simply the religious way of apprehending and interpreting happenings which accompany what is believed to be a Divine Manifestation: whether this mode of interpretation is not essentially 'rationalistic' and entirely conditioned by the scientific presuppositions, or the 'psychology', of the percipient.

We do already discriminate between the miracles recorded in the Gospels. Some of our staunchest apologists have been accustomed to speak of some of them as 'less well attested' than others—words which in the connexion in which they are used must be intended to mean 'less credible'. The Cursing of the Fig-tree is called an 'acted parable'—a comforting phrase which really leaves things just as they were; though in this case the authority of one of the evangelists themselves might be claimed, for the miracle was too difficult for St. Luke, and, though it was in the source before him, he substituted for it the parable of the Barren Fig-tree. But, leaving the Fourth Gospel on one side, this is the only sign we have of any discrimination on the part of the evangelists; and the fact that apologists to-day do commonly discriminate shews how different our mental environment is from that of the witnesses and historians on whose accounts our tradition is based.

Some sixty years ago, Dr. Westcott summoned us to cease to base belief in the Christian Revelation on the evidence of the Miracles by which, as he believed, it was attended, and rather to regard them as parts of the Revelation itself. But he never made clear what it was that they revealed as to the ways in which GOD actually works in the world, or as to the actual conditions, spiritual, moral, or physical, under which as long as we are in the world we must live, so that we should be justified in relying on GOD to succour us in our need in similar ways.

It is not a very long step from Dr. Westcott's position if the next generation, with fresh materials and fresh methods of study of Christian *origines*, find in the 'miracles' of the Gospels 'interpretation' of the Revelation rather than the Revelation itself, and value the narratives as the ways in which believers explained in part the Personality of Him with whom they associated, in all its supernatural intensity and stimulus, the religious experience of which they were conscious.

If in every story of a miracle we see the interpretation of a real experience between the souls of men and GOD, then we have historical continuity of religious belief and faith with those men of the first generation of Christians, and we can use their language as readily as, whether we are Copernicans or Bergsonians, we both think and speak in Ptolemaic terms. The supreme fact for our faith is that Jesus was such a Person as could attract to Himself all that was highest and best in the religious belief of the time; He could centralize and direct it; and peasants and philosophers alike found in Him the realization of their hopes, and applied to the interpretation and expression of their new experience the ideas which they already had. The twentieth century has its prepossessions or presuppositions. So beyond question had the first; and the Christian of that period used the language of his time. He conceived of GOD as free and able to do anything, and of His action in the world under the category of Miracle. And then, as it has been later, the common Christian attitude to Miracle was the same as that of Athanasius in his *Life of Antony*, of whom miracles as remarkable as any in the Gospels were recorded—and believed. It was 'religious' to believe as much as possible; to scrutinize the evidence was impious. The strength of this 'Christian' prejudice in our own time is seen in the readiness with which devout people have accepted the story of 'the Angels of Mons', and having once accepted it have shut their eyes to the fact that the story first appeared in an evening newspaper and that the author has told us that it was a work of purely literary imagination. This story shews us how rapidly, even in the twentieth century, a 'miraculous' interpretation of a remarkable event can win currency among 'religious' people, and become for them inextricably blended with the historical fact itself.

Of course the Christian philosopher of to-day cannot dispense, any more than the simplest believer can, with belief in GOD'S freedom. But order and unity are also conceptions without which he cannot think. And as modern religious thought is influenced more and more by belief in the immanence of GOD in the universe, and recognizes more fully the actual conditions of His work in Nature and in the whole process of the world, the antithesis 'natural and supernatural' loses much of the force it has had. So that, while we still speak of 'miracle', and of GOD'S 'interposition' or 'intervention' in human affairs, we shall wish to be understood to express our belief none the less in His constant Presence and continuous activity, by which He is always bringing new things to pass. If we know, or if we do not know, how it is done, we shall not the less believe that it is He who does it. We shall believe that He works in the world to-day as He always has worked, and that He worked in the past as He works to-day. We shall not think it 'religious' to ignore the evidence either of our senses or of our reason, or to accept as literally true, because they come to us as expressions of a true religious experience, stories of events which in their details seem to us to lack sufficient attestation. We shall apply, in the study of the history of our religion, the canons which we apply in all our historical studies; and the truth of the religious experience itself we shall verify by the only means of verification which Religion admits.

As Christians we stand on the solid rock of this early Christian experience, the same yesterday, to-day, and—as we believe—for ever. The central fact for us is that through Jesus, crucified under Pontius Pilate, men were convinced that they came to know the living GOD; and one by one and in fellowship together they realized a new power of life, a new way of living, present and actual, Regeneration, Redemption, or whatever the name might be by which they called it. This primitive Christian experience is the historical basis of all our doctrines, none of which is of religious value except so far as it mediates this experience to us.

This experience, as regards the personality of our Lord, was most simply interpreted by St. Paul in the words "GOD was in Christ reconciling the world to Himself", or in the words of the Fourth Gospel "He that hath seen me hath seen the Father", or, from another point of view, in the narrative of the Nativity which supplies the formula of the Apostles' Creed as regards the mode of His entrance on human life. Yet other points of view are represented, and other interests served, by the phrases of the opening verses of the Fourth Gospel, by the Epistle to the Hebrews, and by the terms of the Nicene and the Athanasian Creeds. They are all different ways of interpreting or expressing the same religious conviction, and Christians must be allowed some liberty of choice among them.

If we believe that Jesus our Lord, and the whole of His life on earth from its beginning to its end, was a manifestation in history of the Spirit of GOD, of His Personality, His purpose and will, His very Nature and Being, as it can be shewn to men under the conditions of human life—if we share this early Christian conviction and construe the terms of our Creeds in this their religious sense; then we preserve in our use of them true continuity, historical and spiritual, with the first generations of Christians. We mean what the Church has always meant, and the Gospel we have, for ourselves and the world, is the same.

In conclusion, there is a question which it is impossible to pass over, though the full consideration of it would require more space than is now available.

Mr. C. G. Montefiore has lately discussed the question whether 'Liberal' Judaism can take the place of 'Orthodox' Judaism with the 'democracy'[1] (*Liberal Judaism and Hellenism*, Macmillan & Co., 1918). Impressive and attractive as his writing is, I do not find the essay dealing with this question as convincing as some others in his interesting book. Perhaps only a Jew can rightly gauge the force of his argument on this point, so far as it concerns the prospects of Liberal Judaism among the Jewish members of the democracy. But Mr. Montefiore

[1] Mr. Montefiore means by this term the *demos*, the 'working classes', the 'masses'. I have used instead the expression 'the multitude', meaning by it the people as a whole in contrast with the few whose education has been more specialized or 'academic', like Mr. Montefiore's and that of many 'liberal' Christians. But I deem it highly important for this discussion to recognize the fact that many of 'the masses' are, intellectually, quite as competent to understand the liberal position, whether of Jews or of Christians, as are the more 'educated' classes; and the dividing line between them is, for these purposes, very thin and tending to vanish.

also looks forward to a future in which Liberal Judaism will have become a world religion, and it is of course inevitable that a Christian should feel that no form of Judaism (even when enriched in some respects as Mr. Montefiore would enrich it from Christian sources) can ever become the religion of the world, and that the future must belong to Christianity in which the best fruits of the old and unmixed (or already partially Hellenized) Judaism were embodied. Yet any Christian reading Mr. Montefiore's book is sure to be struck by the analogy, both as to present relations and as to future prospects, between 'Liberal' and 'Orthodox' Judaism on the one hand, and 'Liberal' and 'Orthodox' Christianity on the other hand; and, as one of the objections brought against Liberal Christianity is that it can never be a religion for the multitude, it may be useful to note how far the analogy holds good. In many respects it is close, and considerations that apply to the one case apply also to the other.

But there is at least one fundamental and overwhelming difference. It is the difference between loyalty to a Law and loyalty to a Person. The position which Christ occupies in Christianity is *sui generis* and almost wholly distinct from that which Moses has occupied in Judaism. I do not conceive that any Jew has ever felt himself bound

to Moses by the intimate personal bond that binds
all Christians to Christ, and in Him to one another.
To Liberal Jews Moses is a much less important
part of Judaism than he was to Jews before the
new historical perspective had been won—Moses
and the constitution connected with his name.
But the critical study of the Gospels and of the
beginnings of the Christian Religion, and the later
history of Christian thought and institutions—which
is largely responsible for the present cleavage
between 'liberal' and 'orthodox' Christians—tends
to enhance rather than to detract from the religious
significance and the practical appeal of the Person
and Life and the ideals of Jesus. He remains for
Liberal Christianity, quite as truly and as fully as
for Orthodox Christianity, the centre and the
rallying-point. If for some liberal Christians He
is no longer GOD in quite the same sense as He
is for orthodoxy, yet to them too He has the 'value'
of GOD. He is to them as attractive and loveable,
as determinative and adorable a personality, as ever.
For all the purposes of life and thought they
reverently and gratefully own Him in His own
sphere their Master and their Lord, in the full
sense of these high titles. It is to Him that they
are drawn, to Him that they try to reach, to Him
that they make it their ambition to be loyal, to
His feet that they would fain bring others. Service

to Him, in His spirit, is their aim—fellowship with Him the highest prize as well as the motive of their lives. It is from Him that they seek inspiration and renewal. Faith in His GOD and His ideals they believe to be 'the victory that overcometh the world'. This sense of personal and inmost relation of the Christian to the historical Jesus, the ever-living and potent Christ, triumphs over every danger of disruption, and secures a vital continuity of faith that is paramount over and throughout all changes and developements that might seem to involve a breach. Liberal Judaism, I conceive, has no such link with the past, no such continuity as this, to shew, nor any banner like the Christ reigning from the Cross to which to rally mankind for its march to the achievement of its highest good. The analogy between the different schools of Judaism and Christianity fails in this respect.

And there is another important difference. Mr. Montefiore is at pains to consider how Liberal Judaism can retain some of its most ancient and historically characteristic institutions. Christianity, like Judaism, has had institutions from its earliest days, and even dietary regulations, though the latter in comparison with those of Judaism have been few and insignificant. But there is already established among Christians a wide tolerance of differences of opinion as to the *rationale* of these institutions and regulations, and of differences of practice in the observance of them. The dietary regulations, whether by authoritative dispensation or by general consent, are already so frequently or so widely inoperative, among Western Christians at all events, that no case could lie against Liberal Christianity if it entirely ignored them. Of some of the institutions the liberal theory is far from being the same as the orthodox, and some associations of Christians —orthodox in other respects — have deliberately rejected or ceased to use institutions to which others attach importance; but liberal Christians usually value the institutions of their Church as highly, and observe them as fully, as the orthodox; even though the account they would give of them may be different. They have no thought of a Christianity without institutions or needing to apologize for those it has, and there is likely to be in the future far more general agreement than there has been for centuries past, both as to what institutions are of the first importance, and as to the sanctions on which they rest. In respect of institutions, accordingly, there is little danger of any serious cleavage in the future between Liberal and Orthodox Christianity, or of any breach of continuity in the institutional life of the Church as a whole.

Liberal Christianity, accordingly, seems to be equipped both for its own defence in relation to

Orthodox Christianity and for its world-wide 'offensive'—its propaganda to all races and peoples and all sorts and conditions of men—as Liberal Judaism is not and cannot be; and in this respect, whatever prospects of world dominion may lie before Liberal Judaism or Liberal Christianity respectively, their relations to their own domestic orthodoxies are not analogous. Liberal Christianity retains all the features of Orthodox Christianity which are most arresting and impressive to the multitude, and retains them as living and invigorating characteristics of the Gospel which it puts before the world and the life to which it summons men. It is not in any sense a new Faith, but a new interpretation of old beliefs connected with an old Faith; and this fact must control our estimate of the potentialities of Liberal Christianity with all sorts and conditions of men.

The question before us, therefore, is this. Can the view, expressed in these pages, of the relation between the constant and permanent faith of a Christian and the beliefs which have been the concomitants of that faith in the past be expected to commend itself to the mass of believers to-day, and to become naturalized in the Church of the future? At the moment probably the mass of believers in Christianity would answer No. They are so ill informed as to the history of belief and thought in the Church in the past that they are not aware of the chasm that separates them from the beliefs their forefathers associated with various articles of the Creed. They readily suppose that the sense in which such articles are commonly taken to-day—apparently a 'literal' sense—is the sense they always had, and some of their teachers encourage them to think so. They simply do not know that, for example, the belief in 'the resurrection of the body' has been for most orthodox Christians as thoroughly emptied of its original meaning as they will be disposed to think the clause "conceived by the Holy Ghost, born of the Virgin Mary" is by any one who uses it 'merely' as an expression of his faith in the Incarnation. The consideration urged by the Bishop of Oxford that one of these beliefs refers to the future (and therefore may easily be amended and adapted to new knowledge) while the other refers to the past (and therefore stands fixed and unamendable) does not touch the fact that the one belief was as real as the other. The belief in our Lord's miraculous birth does not really rest on any more verifiable experience than the belief in the resurrection of the body. Each belief is biographical, the one relating to the manner in which our Lord's life on earth in the past was conceived to have begun, the other to the manner in which our own lives in the future are conceived to begin and continue. Each belief involves a stupendous miracle as to which no cogent testimony of experience is forthcoming. I see no reason to doubt that the one belief may as easily become obsolete as the other, without any loss of the faith which each embodied in the past.

Again, we are told that the multitude craves miracles. Does it? No doubt we all should like to-day, in our own time and in our own interest, miracles of the kind that 'do not happen'; but I doubt whether the multitude attaches much importance to the miracles supposed to have happened nineteen centuries ago. The miracles that really happen to-day, of a moral and spiritual kind, are much more convincing testimony of the power of the spirit of Christ than any miracles in the physical sphere could be. And if the multitude is to be won to the Christian Religion, it is not likely to be because of miraculous occurrences in the past, but rather because it sees that those who profess its faith are applying that faith increasingly and effectively to the conditions of common life as it is in the world.

The multitude is in fact, I believe, much more intelligent and in closer touch with reality than are many of its would-be 'Christian' teachers and guides; and there is little reason to suppose that the educated democracy of the future will demand or respond to a Religion which purports to offer credentials from a dim and distant past that claim to overawe by their very impossibility and absurdity. I refer to Tertullian's epigram because the same line of appeal is being revived to-day in reaction against the supposed excesses of modern intellectualism in Religion. I do not believe that the masses of the people will ever in the future be held by a Religion which in any way disparages the intellect of man as a means of arriving at the truth of things, and one of the chief channels through which the Spirit of GOD works in the world and reveals the purpose of life. But in any case, in the doctrine of the Incarnation, arrived at independently of the old beliefs expressed in the Creed, there remains a faith emotional enough to satisfy any devotee of unreason in religion—incredible enough to appeal to the dullest imagination—and an ideal attractive enough to win the hearts and potent to direct the wills of men; and both are fused and vitalized in the personal relation of believers to the Person in whose life the impossible was actualized and the ideal embodied and achieved. "He was made man that we may be deified." There is surely enough there. Faith in the Incarnation, interpreted in terms of personality and fellowship, can never be a prosaic or lifeless Creed. It spreads its ramifications into every nook and cranny of human thought and feeling, it throws light on the darkness and goes far to transfigure the struggle and the pain of life. It touches the springs of action and gives both motive and assurance. Just in proportion as it is allowed free course and its moral implications are realized, it tends to create a type of personality and of social order in which the 'democracy' will readily recognize the ideal after which it is groping. The democracy of to-day is Christian in its valuation of personality and its conception of a regenerate human society; but it is not 'orthodox' in its beliefs, and there is no chance of its ever becoming 'orthodox' in the sense in which the word has been used in the past. When it gains a truer historical perspective it may learn to respect the old orthodoxy, as liberal Christians respect it; but it was while the old orthodoxy reigned that the multitude of all classes was lost to the Church, and it is probable that only the new interpretation of the old beliefs can win them to Christ and preserve the Faith of a Christian as the religion of the new era, the dawn of which is already flushing the future with hope.

X

THE CROSS THE SYMBOL OF THE INCARNATION[1]

"YE search the Scriptures, because ye think that in them ye have eternal life; and these are they which bear witness of me; and ye will not come to me, that ye may have life."—St. John v. 39, 40.

If these were our Lord's own words, there is deep pathos in them. The 'Jews' to whom they are spoken acclaim the authority of their Scriptures and look for 'the Hope of Israel'. And He, the speaker, as He is depicted in the Fourth Gospel, fully conscious from the first that He is the mysterious Person to whose coming the Scriptures pointed, as the foreordained Deliverer of His people, cannot deliver them because they will not come to Him. For all their searching of the Scriptures they cannot recognize in Him the Deliverer. And

[1] A sermon preached before the University of Cambridge on Sunday, June 8, 1913.

so in the fulness of the times God's gracious purpose is frustrated. They miss the eternal life that is offered them. The pathos is none the less deep because it was so natural, almost inevitable, that study of the Scriptures should have led them to look for a Saviour of Israel different in all the external conditions of his career on earth from the Prophet of Nazareth. As we read our Gospels to-day we see that He Himself had to learn by experience what He was, and school Himself to believe that what was coming was God's will; and we know that after the events His most devoted disciples needed His Spirit — the sense of His presence with them — to open out to them the Scriptures, before they could collect together their *testimonia* and be convinced that they really bore witness of the actual facts as they had known them.

But, as the words are given by St. John, they are also tinged with irony. Throughout his Gospel he writes of Jesus rather as Christians have come to know Him than as they knew Him in His lifetime. He cares for the 'facts' of the past only so far as he can find in them illustrations, 'signs', of the present, the timeless, reality. And if there be in his Gospel echoes of later controversy with the Jews, we may perhaps hear in them to-day the timeless eternal note that sounds a warning

THE INCARNATION AND THE CROSS 199

to us. For we too have our Scriptures, and our controversies.

The Jews were close students of their Scriptures, unfeignedly believing them: and they failed to find in them the Christ as He was when He came. They had formed from the Scriptures a wrong conception of what He was to be, and therefore they could not accept Him. He 'ought to have been' different.

We too have our own special Scriptures, which to us above all others bear witness of the Christ— our Gospels, which we believe to be inspired just because they tell the history of the past, not merely as it might have seemed to the ordinary on-looker at the time, but in terms of its eternal significance. They interpret it. We can trace the course of the interpreting Spirit of GOD in its ordered progress from St. Mark, through St. Luke and St. Matthew, to its goal in St. John.

And the question presses upon us whether many of those who do not receive the Christ as Saviour and Lord to-day cannot receive Him because they have formed, from the Scriptures, a wrong conception of what He was in His life in the world. This is the one question, vital alike for scholarship and for religion, that gives importance to our modern critical study of the Gospels. Is it the case that the writers of our Gospels themselves felt that He 'must have been' other than He was?

For our knowledge of what He has been ever since to mankind, our knowledge of what He is to-day, we do not depend on our Scriptures. For that we have evidence so vast and varied in its amount and in its ramifications, reaching, as it does, to every nook and cranny of human life for nineteen centuries, that no historian's pen could write it down—the *gesta Christi* in the history of the world, what He has done and what He is doing now. And he who would try to write it would need besides to add the record of all that which no human eye can ever more than dimly discern—the secret history of souls of disciples, learners of Christ—what they aspired to be, all they could never be.

But for our knowledge of what Jesus was in His life on earth, as we call the few years He spent in visible form as one of ourselves among us, for that we depend almost entirely on the Gospels. And our modern critical study of the Gospels leads us—those of us who engage in it wholeheartedly—to a conception of the nature of early Christian experience in which we find new certitude for faith in the Incarnate Son of GOD, but also to a new conception of the conditions of His life in the world in the days in which—in the words of the Fourth Gospel—He "was not yet glorified".

When I speak of our modern critical study of the Gospels, I do not mean what is called a 'moderate' criticism; as though it were an unsavoury remedy or prophylactic to be administered in tiny doses—or as if this were a matter in which a little knowledge might be useful, but much knowledge were a dangerous thing. It may seem so to some of those who feel themselves to be peculiarly the guardians of a great religious tradition, in the light of which our forefathers found their way securely through the maze of life. But to the student of Christian *origines*, the student, not of a mere philosophy, but of a historical religion, whose business it is age after age to study afresh the historical basis of his religion,—to him the phrase 'a moderate criticism' is, I must be allowed in this pulpit to say, thoroughly unscientific, if not absurd. If the method of study which the word describes is not a sound one, not one that may be trusted to lead him to true results, it is his duty to abjure it *in toto*: for truth is his only aim, and to truth there is no smooth, broad, 'moderate' road. But if the method is sound, then he must follow it to the end, quietly and steadily, with loyalty unfailing—if it may not always be unfaltering. For, if anywhere, it is in the process, stage by stage, that danger for the student lurks, as here and there a feature of the traditional portrait suffers change, and the sense of strangeness comes over him and he wonders if really the words "They have taken away my Lord" will be forced from him at the end.

I speak, of course, not of the antiquarian, but of the Christian student, who believes that he has in his Scriptures eternal life, and has it in Him of whom they witness — the student whose belief in the Inspiration of Scripture, whose unfeigned belief in the Bible as the record of the progressive Revelation of GOD, of a real though progressive redemption, which culminated in the Person and Work of our Lord Jesus Christ, compels him to study the record, with all the diligence and knowledge he can bring to bear upon it, in order to know what the revelation, the redemption, is. The story of our Lord's life is set before him by the providence of GOD in different forms. An amalgamation of them all gives him a composite picture which no one has ever been able to see as a whole, except through a veil, dim and majestic, far off: but these or those features of which men and women and children have found unveiled for their eyes, and have learnt to revere and love the Person they inferred from them. What is called the Catholic Faith of the Councils is an attempt to delineate the picture as a whole in words. It comes to us as the work of bishops and scholars ; to whom no doubt it is safer to leave such definitions,

THE INCARNATION AND THE CROSS

for they may be expected to know what they mean : and they at least may be trusted not to tear the picture from its setting—its background of Christian endeavour, its atmosphere of prayer and worship, the lights and the shadows of the movement of life —the ever-changing and yet ever-constant common Christian life, apart from which the definitions of the Church are mere dead bones, its doctrine of the Person of our Lord a patchwork of contradictions.

Even to those who have shared this common life it is probable that the doctrine in its entirety, as defined by the bishops in Council, has seldom been a living present reality. Their allegiance has been given to the gracious, mysterious, indefinable Person pourtrayed in the Gospels. They have needed no narrower definition ; and they rest in peace.

But the critical student of the Gospels is forced to define : to sift the narratives by comparison, to discriminate sources, take account of differences, gauge their significance, weigh their historical values.

And in work of this kind a 'moderate criticism' makes chaos of the old order, the old foundations of belief, without being able to relay the stones out of which the new structure may be reared. What it concedes with one hand it tries all the time to take back with the other. It flies the white flag over positions tenaciously defended in the past, but it occupies them still, and now and again fires a shot from them—into the void. And so it gives the impression that they are still defences of the Faith, and that something vital to the Faith is endangered when they are abandoned : and it hinders the faithful from sallying out into the open, where they can bring all their forces into action.

These old defences, nobly as they served our forefathers, seem to many of our students to-day as ineffectual as the Martello towers on our southern coasts.

In detail there may be much to amend in our method of study, and fresh discoveries may correct some of our results. But one conclusion of profound significance has been reached, on which it is impossible that we students should go back. It is that all our Gospels in varying degrees, but all of them in some degree, have been influenced by later Christian experience in the record that they give us of the 'facts' of our Lord's life.

A rich experience of what Jesus had shewn Himself to be in the world, since He was taken from it, lies behind the portraiture of Him in the Gospels, professedly as He was in His lifetime.

It is the business of the student who would know what He really did and said, what He thought about Himself, the impression He actually produced at the time, to distinguish, wherever he can, the colouring of this later experience, in order to see and come to

THE INCARNATION AND THE CROSS

know the Person as He was. And it is surely a task from which no believer need shrink who is not afraid to know 'Christ after the flesh'—afraid, that is, to pay more than lip-homage to what has always been the peculiar glory of the Christian Creed.

> So, through the thunder comes a human voice
> Saying, O heart I made, a heart beats here!

We are not Jews or Greeks that this peculiar glory of the Christian's Creed should be to us in the twentieth century a stumbling-block or folly. We know that no doctrine that treats the Cross as merely an incident in an *otherwise Divine* career can claim to be anything but a travesty of the Faith that overcame and overcomes the world.

The shadow of the Cross in the Carpenter's shop at Nazareth, if only the artist had painted it luminous instead of dark, would have been a true symbol of the Doctrine of the Incarnation. It was figured in the manger at Bethlehem, as other painters have shewn it, more really than, perhaps, they meant.

The question whether the Atonement is not to be found in the Incarnation itself, rather than in the Cross, divided Christians in former times; and, I believe, it divides them still. But the problem is solved, it melts away, for those who have learnt to see in the Incarnation a life which was all a Passion, all an emptying of self, a humiliation, a real coming down to the level of human life—a real living through a real human experience, the true πάθος μάθος: the life of One who was content by the process of Incarnation to undergo "a sleep and a forgetting", and in His own Person first to realize, before He taught it to us all, that He that is willing to lose Himself shall bring Himself to life, that the Cross which is really redemptive is taken up at birth and borne through life.

The Cross with its 'humiliation', with its reversal of all human judgements and values, is only the symbol of the conditions of our Lord's whole life on earth—the symbol of the utter abasement of the Son of GOD to the limitations of human life.

But it is the risen, the 'glorified', Jesus, who was for the Fourth Evangelist in particular perhaps, but also for the others, and has been ever since, the object of Christian Faith, the centre of Christian experience. In the light of this later 'glorification' St. John interprets the historical Person, whose actual life in the world only shewed 'signs' of what He was. This 'glorification' has cast its light backwards over the whole of the Gospel narrative.

How should it not? We ourselves 'idealize', as we say, those we admire and love—sometimes happily in their lifetime—and by doing so help them to be their best, *possunt quia posse videntur*: and anyhow when we have lost them. They did not know themselves, they did not know what they were to us, we

THE INCARNATION AND THE CROSS 207

ourselves hardly knew. But they actually *were* what they were and are *to us*. And no one who would write their history truly can ignore this intimate judgement of their worth. It must control the final interpretation of their persons.

How much more so in the case of our Lord! 'our GOD Jesus Christ', who, as Ignatius wrote, " now that He is in the Father, is the more plainly manifest", who after His death could make His presence felt as no one else who ever trod this earth. St. John, in describing Jesus as having been always what He was to him and the circle of Christians to which he belonged, was writing history of the highest order— 'inspired' history, as I have said—but not that lower kind of history which the historical student of the Gospels seeks to recover.

I remember hearing from this pulpit years ago, from one whom I recall to-day, as bound to him by many ties of loyalty and affection, one grown old in Christian faith and life, a pathetic and almost passionate plea for the belief of his boyhood that the whole of the book Isaiah was written by the son of Amoz. If it were not so, he said, he would be robbed of the words which he trusted would comfort him as he passed through the shadow of death. That shadow was dark, as I know, in some of its stages, when it came ; but I do not believe that the light which gleamed through it, the light of trust in the

Lord Jesus Christ, whom he had striven to serve, the light of faith in Him as Saviour, was in any degree dependent on the name or the date of the prophet, the truth of whose vision of faith and hope was confirmed, as he believed and we believe, by the Incarnation of the Son of GOD. The prophetic vision was real, whenever, however, it came: and just so far as we can treat it as real we are masters of life, the life that is and is to be.

The evolution—for I believe that the change was orderly rather than catastrophic—the evolution of the conception of prophecy, which the new views as to the composition of the book 'Isaiah' brought with them, was more profound than many of those who lived through it have realized. But the utterances of the prophets have lost none of their power because they are brought into nearer relation to human experience, religious experience at its height. Portent that would compel belief, and left us puzzled rather than impressed, gives place to appeal—the appeal that wins its way to human hearts because it is the outcome of a human experience that knows the pain of life and yet is sure of GOD.

And I cannot doubt that the evolution of the conception of the conditions of our Lord's life on earth, which is coming with our fresh study of the Gospels, will enhance the appeal that the living Christ is making to us in these our times—His times. As we realize more fully the extent to which the Son of GOD 'emptied Himself' to enter on a really human life, to learn from all the experiences 'of joy and woe, and hope and fear', with no supernatural panoply to blunt the edge of any one of them that each of us may not obtain—the appeal He makes to us will not be less persuasive and convincing than of old. We shall not have the strange spectacle, which we have to-day, of the learned gravely arguing for or against the very existence of a historical Jesus. Elusive as His personality in its fulness remains, no one will doubt that He, the hem of Whose vesture he can touch, was a real Person, very Man, though unique among men—One who can be the Example and Guide and Saviour of men, because He first found and trod the path through life unto life Himself, that so they might have life, and have it abundantly.

We may read the Fourth Gospel, and parts of the other Gospels, less as the expression of the consciousness of Jesus Himself in His life in the world, and more as the record of early Christian experience, the reflexion of the impression He made, what He actually was to believers of the first and the second generation, what they had found Him to be *to them* in their own experience—the Way, the Truth, and the Life, the Resurrection, the newborn life in this life, the Light of the World. Do the words come to us with less appeal if they are not claims or promises made by our Lord, but quiet statements of the conviction of disciples that the acceptance of Him as the Christ, the Son of GOD, had actually resolved for them the enigma of the world and themselves? Do they come to us to-day with less 'authority' if they are not sayings of Jesus about Himself to win men to Him, but the ascription to Him by others already won of the titles which expressed the simple facts—the wonderful facts—as they knew them in their own moral and spiritual experience?

We shall not, of course, forget that it was the historical Person who produced this impression, Whoever, whatever, He was. And the impression has never died out. It has been renewed in experience age after age. Our doctrines and Creeds were designed to preserve it, ever fresh, as a power in the world. If at any time they cease to serve this purpose; if they obscure this primitive impression, as for some undoubtedly they do to-day; if men go to others rather than to Him in their quest of the Way, the Truth, and the Life; kept from Him by the expressions of the faith and piety of former days: then, if at all they may be re-won, it will be by that very process of fearless study—reverent and patient of course, as all true study, whatever the matter of the study is, must always be—

reverent and patient and free—that very process of study of early Christian experience, enshrined in its manifold forms in the Gospels, which to-day is the terror of some and a new revelation to others.

And if they cannot find exactly what Jesus was, they will have come to know Him as they can know Him in no other way. They will scarcely trouble to ask whether He is or is not the Person of the Creeds. They will have come to Him, and they will have life.

THE END

Printed by R. & R. CLARK, LIMITED, *Edinburgh*.

www.ingramcontent.com/pod-product-compliance
Lightning Source LLC
Chambersburg PA
CBHW060600230426
43670CB00011B/1910